G000042576

Written by Jim Drewett & Alex Leith, Deadline Features
Design by Andy Smith
Text research by Clive Batty
Picture research by Justyn Barnes • Thanks to Ben at Action Images
Statistical research by Louise Pepper
Sub-edited by Nicky Hodge

Photographs by: John Peters, Action Images, Colorsport,
News Team International, John D Jones, Cliff Butler
Thanks to: Fergie for lending us his personal photo album
and to Lyn Laffin

First Published in 1996 by Manchester United Books
an imprint of André Deutsch Ltd, 106 Great Russell Street, London, WC1B 3LJ
in association with Manchester United Football Club Plc, Old Trafford, Manchester, M16 ORA
Copyright © 1996 Manchester United Football Club

CIP data for this is available from the British Library

ISBN 0233 99047 X

Printed in Italy

A Zone Production

Alex Ferguson

Ten Glorious Years
1986–1996
by Jim Drewett & Alex Leith

ANDRE
DEUTSCH

**Above left: former United favourite Brian Kidd was recruited to ensure the best youngsters
came to the club. In 1991 he became Alex's assistant manager.
Above centre: Sir Matt Busby still watches proudly over Old Trafford.
Above right: that man Cantona scores the goal that beat Liverpool in the 1996 FA Cup Final.**

LITTLEWOODS

troduction

by Alex Ferguson

"On 17 November 1986, I was appointed manager of Manchester United Football Club. After 10 fantastic years at Aberdeen, it was time for a fresh challenge. And at United (the only club I would ever consider leaving Pittodrie for), I certainly found one."

"Suddenly I was in the hotseat of the biggest club in Britain (maybe the biggest in Europe, maybe even the world). A club that hadn't won the League title for an unbelievable 20 years. A club where attendances had plummeted and there was next to no cash available for transfers... Well, no one ever said life was supposed to be a bed of roses.

"Ten years later, I sit in my office at Old Trafford safe in the knowledge that the Premiership trophy and the FA Cup are safely locked up on display just down the corridor. But as I sit at my desk, I have no desire to look back on past triumphs. I'm not one for crowing. My job is to maintain the standards we have set ourselves over the last few years, standards that the United supporters rightly expect of this great club. If we don't win at least one trophy a year then we are not doing our jobs, and my past record will speak for nothing. 'Laurel-resting' is not listed in the hobbies section of the Alex Ferguson fact-file.

"I am proud to be Manchester United's longest-serving manager since Sir Matt Busby. Looking back over the years, I'm encouraged to think that my own career at Old Trafford has started to go down a similar road to my great predecessor's. Sir Matt's first trophy was the FA Cup in 1948, as was mine in 1990. A few seasons later, like me, he won the League Championship after finishing second a few times. Europe is another avenue Sir Matt went down with distinction and another hurdle that I have overcome – although not yet in the European Cup. Sir Matt created the Busby Babes and I'm certainly trying my utmost to bring on our own young players again.

"When you study his career you can see his plans unfolding. It's marvellous to behold. He wasn't just living from day to day. He had an overall strategy that, by 1955, saw him produce a brilliant team, only to see it destroyed three years later in the Munich air crash, before the side could reach its peak. He had bought players, but only to add to a nucleus of talent he had found and nurtured. My aim, with Sir Matt very much in mind, is to maintain the club's reputation and tradition, and to do what I can to win at least one trophy every year.

"Since my appointment I have tried to embrace and then master the unique challenge of taking the helm at Manchester United. Every aspect of the club – from the creation of a youth policy, through the overhaul of the players' diet and appointment of a club chaplain, to the signing of the top stars in world football – has been thoroughly scrutinised. I have made it my business to leave no stone unturned in my determination to put this club back at the very top... and then keep it there.

"After a barren start, it has been fantastic in recent years to be able to bring trophies back to United. Together with my years at St Mirren and Aberdeen, I am proud of the successes of these 10 seasons at United: three Premiership titles, three FA Cups, a League Cup and a European Cup Winners' Cup.

"Sir Matt made this club and has left me an inheritance and obligation that makes me say to myself: 'I need to manage Manchester United in a very special way.' And I'll keep doing that for as long as Manchester United will have me."

The last manager to bring the League Championship to Old Trafford was the late, great Sir Matt Busby in 1967. Alex Ferguson was well aware that his only true measure of success would be regaining that title.

Fergie's CV

Alex Ferguson was born in Govan, Glasgow, in 1941. Growing up in the tough, working environment of the shipyards where his father plied his trade, he played football in boots handed down from his cousins and dreamed, like all the other kids, of playing for Rangers. Unlike all the other kids, one day he would.

Newlyweds Alex and Cathy in 1967

With a Protestant father and a Catholic mother, young Alex Ferguson had no regard for the sectarian differences that so often divide Glasgow. But when it came to football, his allegiances lay always with the blue half of the city and he would regularly climb over a wall to get into Ibrox – once getting caught by a steward who threatened to tell his mother!

Although nowadays he invariably sidetracks the "what's the secret of your success?" question, get him to talk about his upbringing and its influence is immediately obvious. "I know deep down that it has got to be the naturally hard-working background I come from," he says. "I am proud and happy to say that I had wonderful parents who worked hard and passed on to me the value of that ethic. There was not a lot of money flying about but my background was not poor because you never considered yourself poor."

His father, also called Alex, was a strict disciplinarian. "In the five years of my apprenticeship [as a toolmaker] I was never late once. I can never be late for anything," Ferguson says now, although he claims he is more like his mother than his father. "My mother had fantastic determination," he reflects. And younger brother Martin, once a player with Partick Thistle and St Johnstone, claims: "If I'd had Alex's determination I'm sure I could have done better in football. In fact I'm certain of it."

It was at Govan High School that Ferguson started to believe that his dream of becoming a footballer might come true, when he was selected to play for Glasgow Schools. He'd become both a fearless and fearsome striker; a lethal goalscorer and terroriser of hapless centre halves. As his Rangers colleague John Greig said: "Everybody will tell you he should have worn his football boots on his elbows because he played with them sticking out all the time. He made John Fashanu look like Miss Piggy."

At the age of 16 he was on the books of famous Scottish club Queens Park, while working at the same time as an apprentice toolmaker. Elected also an assistant shop steward, Ferguson didn't hesitate to cast his vote in favour of strike action when a strike was called in 1960.

Back on the football pitch he made his debut for Queens Park in 1958, scoring 11 goals in 31 league games. He then moved on to St Johnstone in 1960 (22 goals in 45 league games); Dunfermline in 1964 (66 goals in league 88 games) and then to his beloved Rangers in 1967 for a record £60,000.

For 'the Gers' he kept up his phenomenal scoring record (35 in 67 games – he was top scorer every year at every club he played for), but he was sent off almost as often as he scored for anything from dangerous play to dissent. "Every one of them an injustice," jokes Ferguson now of his seven dismissals, "I don't know how it happened."

"He didn't like losing," suggests Greig, "and when he put on the Rangers jersey he was following not only his own ambition but his family's for him to play for Rangers FC. He got involved. He hated losing. It's just a pity he didn't stay longer than he did."

After two years at Ibrox he was offered the chance of becoming player/coach at Falkirk. "I didn't want to leave, but eventually I realised that I had to go," he says. And so the long, hard climb up the managerial ladder began. From Falkirk he moved to Ayr (where he still managed to score 10 goals in 24 games), and then in 1974 he was appointed player/boss of East Stirling.

He soon found out what he'd let himself in for. Two weeks before the start of the season, he discovered that the club had only eight players. "I said: 'Mr Chairman, do you know that you need 11 players to start a bloody game of football?'" He got £2,000 to buy five new players. He was learning.

"When I first started as a manager I was impulsive and impetuous. I wanted to do things without telling or referring to anyone else. As you get the experience, the edges get knocked off, and you're not so vulnerable either.

"I admired Jock Stein tremendously. His great strength was knowing people, knowing their weaknesses. I also learnt a lot from my old Rangers boss Scott Symon. I learnt one thing in particular – never criticise players publicly."

After four-and-a-half months at cash-strapped East Stirling he was lured to St Mirren where his reputation as a ferocious manager spread when he sacked eight players in one day. In 1976/77 he won his first managerial honour, guiding St Mirren to the First Division title and promotion to the Premier League. The following summer he moved to Aberdeen amid much behind-the-scenes wrangling at the St Mirren's ground, inappropriately named Love Street.

What Ferguson went on to achieve at Pittodrie is still one of the most astonishing stories in the history of Scottish football. In 10 glorious years (anyone get a feeling of déjà vu here?), he won the Premier League three times, the Scottish Cup four times (including the double in 1984) and the Scottish League Cup in 1985/86. Moreover, he broke the 'Old Firm' stranglehold on Scottish football (Aberdeen's first title win in 1980 was the first non-Old Firm triumph for 15 years). In 1983 the club won the European Cup Winners' Cup and the European Super Cup.

"People recognised the enormous potential at Aberdeen. Its real strength was its family feeling and team spirit among the players, who had grown up together in the same city." Men like Gordon Strachan, Jim Leighton, Willie Miller, all blossomed under Ferguson's leadership – the secret was having a team of 'winners', the manager always claimed. His then assistant manager, Archie Knox, puts it differently: "Players were left in no doubt that they had to display winner qualities or they were no use to him."

While with Aberdeen, Ferguson took control of the Scotland team for the 1986 World Cup in Mexico, a relatively disastrous trip in which the side lost to Denmark and Germany, drew with Uruguay, and ended up on the first plane home.

"It was a very difficult group. I didn't enjoy it too much, there was a conflict of interest with so many Aberdeen players in the squad and I came home convinced I had to move."

Ferguson and his chairman at Aberdeen, Dick Donald, had an understanding. "I told him I was quitting at the end of the season. I needed a new challenge. He said the only job you should leave for is Manchester United, so we had a sort of agreement that Aberdeen would not stand in my road if United came in for me."

Which is exactly what happened after Ron Atkinson was shown the door at Old Trafford. "It was unanimous that Alex Ferguson was the man," claims the club's chairman Martin Edwards. "My reasons were that he had taken Aberdeen from being a small, relatively unsuccessful Scottish club to challenge the might of Rangers and Celtic."

So on 7 November 1986 it was announced to the world. "My first impression was: 'This is the biggest club in the game,'" remembers Ferguson of his first days in his new office at Old Trafford. "All I could think of was how was it that they hadn't won the league."

He was to change all that...

Far left: giving instructions to Gordon Strachan.
Left: Willie Miller celebrates Aberdeen's 1983 European Cup Winners' Cup success.
Opposite page: Fergie battles with Celtic's Billy McNeil in the 1969 Scottish Cup Final.

Page 18   DAILY RECORD, Tuesday, August 1, 1967

The big Ibrox splashout continues . . .

£55,000 RANGER

Goal promise as Ferguson signs on

RANGERS' mammoth spending spree—they have splashed out £200,000 in a year on the transfer market — may continue today.

After spending a Scottish record fee of £55,000 for Dunfermline's Alex Ferguson yesterday manager Scot Symon revealed Swedish star Orjan Persson may become a Rangers player today or tomorrow.

When Persson joins up at Ibrox the Rangers outlay will almost certainly top the quarter of a million pounds mark.

Determined

After a month of delays and snags in their efforts to land Ferguson and Persson, Rangers are now moving fast in their determined bid to catch up with jet-age Celtic.

Ferguson achieved a life-long

The new hero . . . goal ace Alex Ferguson "signs on" for young autograph hunters out

ambition when he signed yesterday.

For until he got married just over a year ago, Ferguson lived only five minutes away from Ibrox.

" As a kid I was Rangers daft," the jubilant inside forward told me yesterday. "Now I've achieved my ambition.

" Manager Symon told me I'd be playing in Saturday's friendly against Arsenal at Highbury and I'm determined to do well.

The fact that he is the highest-priced player ever to wear the Light Blue won't

By ALISTER NICOL

to score goals—and I aim TO SCORE PLENTY.

" I was very conscious I was playing for a transfer last season and the harder I tried to score the more DIFFICULT it became."

" Now," he went on, " the pressure is off, I'm ready to play my heart out for Rangers."

Advantage

Persson, who notched 95

Ferguson's goal flair to advantage.

And it's as A STRIKER that Rangers will use him. He'll probably take over the No. 9 jersey from former Dunfermline team-mate Alex Smith and stay near goal.

But Fergie is more than a poacher. He's a non-stop TRIER who never knows when he's beaten. He can take plenty rough stuff and, when need be, dish it out.

A true professional, I doubt if any of Rangers' high-priced stars will fight harder for the club than Alex Ferguson.

Although Orjan Persson returned to his home in

Opposite page, above left:
On 31 July 1967, Alex becomes the most
expensive player in Scotland; below left:
Alex, Cathy and kids at home in 1973. Above:
The family reassembled in Aberdeen in 1983
with the European Cup Winners' Cup (left)
and the Scottish Cup (right).
Left: Alex and his Aberdeen team before the
Scottish FA Cup Final in 1983.

A breath

1986/87

Big Ron got the chop and
Fergie (above right) eagerly jumped into the Old
Trafford hotseat.

# of fresh air

On the morning of 6 November 1986, Manchester United fans had every reason to feel annoyed. Their team was languishing in 19th place in the First Division and it felt as if the whole country was taking the mickey out of them. Spirit in the United dressing room had also hit rock bottom. They'd already lost at home to Charlton, West Ham and Chelsea. Memories of relegation in 1974 loomed large. And to cap it all, the team had just been knocked out of the League Cup by Southampton. Not just knocked out, in fact. They'd been thrashed 4-1. Manchester United didn't feel like Manchester United any more. It was time for a change.

It had all looked so good a year earlier, with Ron Atkinson's flamboyant team unbeaten in their first 15 games and seemingly heading for the title, with Strachan, Hughes, Olsen, Stapleton and Robson all in goalscoring form, and 16 league and cup wins already under their belts. Then the bubble burst and United limped home with only nine more league wins all season, dropping a huge lead in the league to finish third, having been knocked out of the League Cup by Liverpool and the FA Cup in the fifth round at home to West Ham.

Something had gone radically wrong for Manchester United, then, and most fans reacted with relief when it was announced on 6 November that Big Ron had been sacked by Chairman Martin Edwards. Having decided on change, Edwards didn't hang around. That same day he rang up Aberdeen chairman Dick Donald to get permission to approach his manager Alex Ferguson, and flew straight to Scotland to meet him. The very next morning Ferguson was at Old Trafford, having signed on the dotted line, to meet the players and press.

You'd imagine that it would've been a tough choice for Ferguson, Aberdeen's most successful ever manager, who'd won 10 trophies at the Granite City club in just eight seasons – including the European Cup Winners' Cup. But not at all. "In my time there I turned down chances to manage Rangers, Arsenal and Spurs, but when the opportunity came to join Manchester United I decided I could no longer stay in my safe house in Aberdeen," he recalls. "I felt I hadn't achieved enough, and once you stop striving in football it's time to chuck it all in. So I was ready, and it didn't take long for me to reach agreement with Martin Edwards."

It was a costly change of management for Edwards and United, who had to pay over £1 million in compensation to Atkinson, his coach Mick Brown, and Aberdeen, as well as a £250,000 contract for their new manager. But Edwards was confident he'd made the right move. "I am sure that we have made a wise choice. We had to move quickly – once we had decided to get rid of Ron we wanted to replace him as quickly as possible," he said after the deal was struck.

Ferguson wasn't under any misapprehensions about what a huge job he had taken on. "I knew all about the record of Manchester United when I decided to quit Aberdeen and take up the challenge of Old Trafford," he says. "I knew it was a club laced with traditions and great expectations." But he didn't quite grasp the complexity of the task in hand, as he explained years later with the benefit of hindsight. "I had no real inklings about the demands. No manager is prepared for the job at Old Trafford. I think it took me three or four years to understand fully the politics and requirements, the demands and pressures." Having won trophies galore in Scotland, he was a little mystified too about all the fuss surrounding United. "When I first arrived, Manchester United seemed a mystery to me. To an outsider it's difficult to understand how a club which didn't win the league could attract such a big following. It was a mystery I wanted to become a part of, though."

Ferguson didn't have long to settle into Old Trafford before the first hurdle appeared. On 8 November, a day after he'd arrived in Manchester, he had to leave again to travel with his team to Oxford United. Manchester United badly needed to win to push their way out of the relegation zone. Fergie got Atkinson's coach Brian Whitehouse, who'd broken the news of Big Ron's departure and the new manager's arrival to the players and staff at the club, to help him pick the team.

In goal was Chris Turner, a former Sunderland keeper, who'd recently won a regular place from the injury-prone Gary Bailey, but wasn't enjoying a fine run of form. The United veterans Mike Duxbury and Arthur Albiston were at full back, with Graeme Hogg and Kevin Moran in central defence. In midfield were Irish international Paul McGrath; Remi Moses, who'd recently been in the news for a training-ground clash of heads with Danish star Jesper Olsen; alongside them were ex-England winger Peter Barnes and Clayton Blackmore. Up front were Peter Davenport, a disappointment since his big-money move from Forest in 1985, and Frank Stapleton, another Irish international who, at the age of 30, was in his fifth season at the club. Olsen was on the bench. Bryan Robson and Norman Whiteside were sidelined with injuries. It was a passable team, but compared with with United teams of the past and with contemporary Liverpool and Everton teams, it was

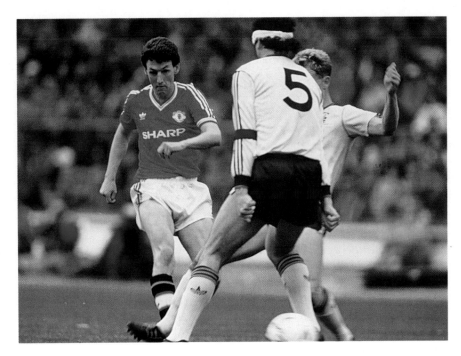

Peter Davenport never reproduced his Nottingham Forest form at United.

definitely not a great one. Nevertheless, Ferguson was upbeat in his pre-match talk to the press. "The league title has got to be the players' objective, and they could even do it this season," he stated. "I have never thought in terms of being second or third. My job is to win every game here. That's the way I intend to attack the job, and I'm sure that the players do not need to be told what the target is."

That day at the Manor Ground, however, the team seemed to lose sight of the target. United lost 2-0. It could hardly be blamed on Ferguson, but it certainly made him aware of the huge task he had on his hands. United stayed second from bottom. Ferguson was furious in the press conference afterwards and the papers had a field day at United's expense. "I watched, studied and then opened my mouth rashly when I would have been wiser to keep it shut. I confessed to the press that the fitness of United's players was poor. I added that the problem would be resolved, and fast," he remembers.

It wasn't just a question of fitness, as Ferguson discovered later. "During the next few weeks I detected deeper, even more alarming truths about the United team I had inherited. We weren't equipped for the occasional rough-house rigours and combative nature of the league at that time. More than anything else, we just could not cope with having both Jesper Olsen and Gordon Strachan in the same side. They weren't physically built to handle the popular football strategy in England at that time." This was the era, remember, when long-ball football was in vogue.

Fergie's immediate response was to introduce longer and harder training methods. His first two important signings brought Archie Knox – his Aberdeen assistant – and Brian Kidd on to his training staff. "I had to look at the standard of fitness at the club and I came to the conclusion that it was simply not good enough. There was no way you could expect the players to compete in 60 battles to the level demanded of Manchester United. They had to be prepared to produce in every game and I don't think they were capable of delivering. Archie, who had always worked like a beast himself, took charge of that aspect."

After a few weeks the new training strategies started working. "There's no doubt about it, things have changed and the players seem to like the way things are being done," said Bryan Robson a few weeks into the Ferguson reign. "I've got to be honest and say that I've never felt stronger in my legs than I feel now. I've had a lot of trouble with my hamstrings but the manager has got me doing different routines to strengthen my legs and they seem to be working."

Results, too, started to pick up. United drew at Norwich the following week, and then beat QPR 1-0 with a goal from John Sivebaek in Ferguson's first game in charge at Old Trafford. After the Oxford match, United lost only two of their next 15 matches and began to claw their way up the table. The season started looking positively healthy around the turn of the year, when United beat Liverpool at Anfield on Boxing Day and Manchester City in the third round of the FA Cup at Old Trafford a couple of weeks later. "Ferguson put his finger on things quickly and made a very good impression – he was like a breath of fresh air," said his veteran defender Kevin Moran.

Ferguson wasn't satisfied however, and made no bones about it to his directors. "After a while I had time to assess the situation and I didn't like what I saw," he says. "When I met the directors at the end of my first half-season I told them we needed nine new players to win the Championship. To put it mildly, I think they were surprised. I think they felt that all they needed was a fresh hand on the tiller, but what concerned me was the fact that there were too many players on the wrong side of 28 or thereabouts. They were too old to go for the challenges I had in mind. Individually, they all still had a lot of football in them, but collectively they added up to a team which, while experienced, had lost the magic spark.

"I looked at all the contracts, ages and the number of games certain players had missed with injury and wondered how long some of them would last. I had to be hard-headed. I suppose Frank Stapleton was the biggest disappointment. Here was a much respected player with four FA Cup winners' medals, two with Arsenal and two with Manchester United. His reputation was as long as your arm, but he had lost his mobility and just didn't look as if he would ever score a goal."

Ferguson also detected another problem that he had to solve, and fast. It was a problem that was manifesting itself not on the pitch, but in the bar afterwards. "There was a lot of drinking going on behind the scenes," says Ferguson. "It seemed to be part of the game here, a social sideshow in which top professionals cannot really afford to be involved. I wondered if it was the pressure of playing for United that created it or whether they felt that, at such a big club, it was the macho thing to do. The one conclusion I came to without any question was that things had to change. I stopped the lunchtime binges and made sure they knew how I felt about that aspect of their lives."

United finished the season in 11th place, after an indifferent run-in at the end of the season. It was their worst League position since they'd been relegated in 1974, but things looked a hell of a lot healthier than they had in November. Fergie had put his finger on the problems at the club, and started to tackle them. Now it was time to start sorting out what happened on the pitch.

The training ground clash between Moses (far left) and Olsen (left) highlighted the turmoil Fergie inherited.

1986/87

Back row: Peter Davenport, John Sivebaek, Gary Walsh, Paul McGrath, Liam O'Brien, Kevin Moran.
Front row: Mike Duxbury, Brian McClair, Bryan Robson, Gordon Strachan, Colin Gibson.

Football League Division One

Nov 29	(a)	Wimbledon	L	0–1	
Dec 7	(h)	Tottenham	D	3–3	Whiteside, Davenport 2
Dec 13	(a)	Aston Villa	D	3–3	Davenport 2, Whiteside
Dec 20	(h)	Leicester C	W	2–0	Gibson C, Stapleton
Dec 26	(a)	Liverpool	W	1–0	Whiteside
Dec 27	(h)	Norwich C	L	0–1	
Jan 1	(h)	Newcastle U	W	4–1	Jackson P, Whiteside, Stapleton, Olsen
Jan 3	(a)	South'ton	D	1–1	Olsen
Jan 24	(h)	Arsenal	W	2–0	Strachan, Gibson T
Feb 7	(a)	Charlton A	D	0–0	
Feb 14	(h)	Watford	W	3–1	McGrath, Davenport,Strachan
Feb 21	(a)	Chelsea	D	1–1	Davenport
Feb 28	(h)	Everton	D	0–0	
Mar 7	(h)	Man City	W	2–0	Reid, Robson
Mar 14	(a)	Luton T	L	1–2	Robson
Mar 21	(a)	Sheff W	L	0–1	
Mar 28	(h)	Notts Forest	W	2–0	McGrath, Robson
Apr 4	(h)	Oxford U	W	3–2	Davenport 2, Robson
Apr 14	(a)	West Ham	D	0–0	
Apr 18	(a)	Newcastle U	L	1–2	Strachan
Apr 20	(h)	Liverpool	W	1–0	Davenport
Apr 25	(a)	QPR	D	1–1	Strachan
May 2	(h)	Wimbledon	L	0–1	
May 4	(a)	Tottenham	L	0–4	
May 6	(a)	Coventry C	D	1–1	Whiteside
May 9	(h)	Wimbledon	W	3–1	Blackmore, Duxbury, Robson

Final League position: 11th in Division One

FA Cup

3rd Round:

Jan 10	(h)	Man City	W	1–0	Whiteside

4th Round:

Jan 31	(h)	Coventry C	L	0–1	

Fergie's

fledglings

It's 1-1 in the 1996 FA Cup semi final against Chelsea. Blues' midfielder Craig Burley mis-hits a back pass and 21-year-old David Beckham is on it like a flash. He beats struggling defender Terry Phelan to the ball, reaches it just inside the box and calmly strokes it past Kevin Hitchcock and into the bottom corner as if he scored semi final winners every day. United are in the FA Cup Final, and 41 days later their Wembley squad will include five players who have come through the club's youth system. Not one of them will be older than 21.

"I've always done it, at every club I've been with. St Mirren had a good youth policy, Aberdeen had an excellent youth policy and now United have an absolutely wonderful youth policy." Alex Ferguson warms to his favourite subject: "I have always considered that the player you produce is better than the one you buy. The development of young players at our club is outstanding. I decided early on in management that it's a commitment that can give you an enormous amount of satisfaction, and build family spirit and team spirit."

When Ferguson arrived at United in 1986, the chances of the club's youth policy producing a team that could win the Zenith Data Systems Cup – let alone the FA Cup – looked pretty slim. In the season that Ferguson arrived at Old Trafford, Manchester City beat United 5-1 in the FA Youth Cup Final. City's team including the likes of David White, Ian Brightwell, Fitzroy Simpson, Paul Lake and Andy Hinchcliffe. There was a serious problem here and Fergie knew it.

"Manchester City was doing better than us. Even Oldham and Crewe were doing better than us. So I called meetings with our scouts and told them I wasn't satisfied with the standard of the youngsters they were bringing to the club. I think they were hurt and shocked but it had to be done. I said they mustn't just bring me the best boy in the street, but the best in the country.

"I took over a system that had 20 scouts in Scotland, yet in Greater Manchester – with a population almost the same size as Scotland – we had only four. One or two of our scouts left, but I couldn't help that." He brought in an extra scout in the North East and started a school of excellence in Durham after enlisting Bryan 'Pop' Robson, the former Newcastle and West Ham player.

In 1987 Ferguson made one of his most important signings. It wasn't a player he enlisted, it was former United and City striker Brian Kidd. Put straight in charge of the club's youth policy, Kidd's brief was simple: "I told him that his mandate was to tie up this area. I didn't want to hear any more about Manchester City getting the best kids'.

"So the ball was rolling. At the beginning we took gambles with players, mainly to let everyone know that Manchester United were back in business. We made sure there was decent coaching for the youngsters. People probably didn't realise that had to be done, but I was experienced in that area because the development of youngsters had been central to Aberdeen's success.

"There are certain things we do for the young players which are important, like providing a dining facility at the training ground to make sure we put the right fuel in their engines. We have two chefs at the training ground, we have a nutritionist who comes in once a week. The food they eat is now excellent. We also want to instil self-discipline into our youngsters, or at least a willingness to accept discipline. If they can't do that then there's no future for them.

"No young player has ever left here voluntarily. We look after young players very well, though we don't pay them a penny. By not offering them money to sign, everyone in the dressing room knows they are getting the same deal. Paying signing-on fees creates envy and breaks up the camaraderie. At that stage they should be playing for love, not money, and anything that sets players against each other is bad for them, bad for the team, and bad for the club. So we just said right from the start: 'If a boy wants to come to the club he'll get the same deal as everyone else.'

"I have a very hands-on approach to the youth system, which also involves the parents. It is particularly important that I know who the young kids are and watch them play in their trials. We think it's important that the family know the manager as well. You always feel the mother might say: 'I wonder if the manager even knows who my son is?' So we make sure that doesn't happen."

United now have three Schools of Excellence – in Manchester, Durham and Belfast (where Keith Gillespie was discovered). By 1992 the new system had produced a team capable of winning the FA Youth Cup... and later much, much more.

"Right from the start of the season I fancied our boys to win the youth competition and they delivered some unbelievably good performances. I spoke with David Pleat at Luton and he said he couldn't believe the

**Young lions: Scholes, Butt, Casper and
Gary Neville, vanguard of England youth.**

quality of our side. He reckoned we would conquer the youth scene in England for the next five years with the players we've got."

The team that beat Crystal Palace to lift the FA Youth Cup that year was Pilkington, O'Kane, Switzer, Casper, Neville G, Beckham, Butt, Davies, Giggs, McKee, Thornley, Savage and Burke. After that match Ferguson said he felt five of the team were capable of "reaching the standard necessary to play in United's first team". He underestimated. Ryan Giggs had already made his first appearance, but so to date have no less than eight of his teammates on that day – plus Phil Neville and Paul Scholes.

"We knew as soon as we saw them play that this group of players could go all the way," recalls Ferguson. "You get cycles of players and this crop are exceptional. I had the same thing at Aberdeen. After a cycle there may be a period where it drops off and you only get ones and twos coming through. Unfortunately, you don't get a constant stream of Nevilles, Butts and Scholes through all the time. That was an absolutely exceptional team, that – possibly the best-ever youth team in English football."

At the beginning of the 1994/95 season Alex Ferguson took a gamble. Success at United had brought its own problems, and one of them was fixture congestion. So on 21 September he decided to put his 'fledglings' in at the deep end in a tricky Coca-Cola Cup tie away at Port Vale. Amid huge controversy over picking a 'weakened' line-up, Ferguson named the following side: Walsh, G Neville, May, Keane, Irwin, Gillespie, Beckham, Butt, McClair, Scholes, Davies. The team won 2-1 and the *Daily Telegraph* crowed: 'If they're good enough, they're old enough'!

"If they have the quality, age is no barrier," says Ferguson. "I have proved that in the past with Sharpe and Giggs, and Mark Robins who jumped the senior queue at no more than 18. But I think it was important that we gave them a chance, to keep the momentum going. We didn't want them to stagnate in the Reserves for too long, because we knew they were going to be first-team players."

After the 2-0 second leg-win over Port Vale that year, Ferguson was quoted as saying: "Overall in the two games, the way the youngsters played served to confirm what I already knew: that they all have real strength. Their technical ability and temperament is good, but what we don't know yet is whether they have the real capacity to go right to the top: to play on the big stages against the best players, in games against teams who are going to man-mark and be rough with them."

Those questions have now been answered, although Ferguson believes in many ways the hard part of his task is just beginning. "You never know about a young player until he's got through the first year and into the second, when he finds himself playing against teams that know him and plan tactics against him. Then you see how they handle it – and handle success – which is the biggest problem for a football manager."

Left: Ryan Giggs scores the 1992/93 goal of the season against QPR at Loftus Road.
Opposite page: the 11-year-old David Beckham wins a soccer skills competition at Old Trafford in 1986.

The

1987/88

Above left: in a year of rebuilding, Ferguson and
Knox bought McClair (above centre) from Celtic.
Above right: Steve Bruce took the long route to
United, via Gillingham and Norwich City.

gardener

The Manchester United that Alex Ferguson had inherited in 1986 was no footballing Garden of Eden. It was an overgrown mess, in fact, which needed a damn good clear-up. He had spent the 1986/87 season wandering round the garden seeing what measures needed to be taken to restore it to its former glory. He looked closely at what he wanted to keep and what he wanted to get rid of, and tried out 23 players in his first seven months in charge. Now was the time for pruning. Pruning and replanting.

On 1 July, during the close season before Fergie's first full term at the club, he made two signings, Viv Anderson and Brian McClair, both of them through league tribunals. Viv Anderson was the cheaper of the two at just £250,000. "I spoke to Don Howe and couldn't have got a better testimony. Bobby Robson was full of praise. I knew he was out of contract that summer and therefore available. He was a marvellous bit of business," says Ferguson of Anderson. The right back was a former England international – the first black player to win a full cap for England – and had grown used to success at Nottingham Forest.

McClair was signed to add a touch of goalscoring bite to the United attack. He'd just scored 35 goals for Celtic, who'd wanted £2 million for his services. He too was out of contract. At £850,000 he looked another snip, and turned out to be just that.

Ferguson knew that he had the resources to get the right players. What was important was getting the right mix, too. "As a manager you must separate the essential from the trivial and pick teams to win matches rather than simply players who you like. There has always got to be a mixture of players in a dressing room. There has to be the studious one, the flamboyant type, the thinker, the battler."

Just before Christmas, after an injury to Paul McGrath, Ferguson felt he had to make another plunge into the transfer market. England international Terry Butcher had all but signed when he broke his leg, so Steve Bruce of Norwich became the manager's new target. Norwich Chairman Robert Chase stalled as much as he could on the deal to try and increase Bruce's price. In the end, after Ferguson had called his bluff and withdrew, Chase relented and Bruce travelled across the country with £800,000 changing hands.

There were sales too: Frank Stapleton went to Ajax and John Sivebaek to St Etienne in the close season. Other players were put on the transfer list. It was time for Fergie to get harsh. "I had a lot of sorting out to do that season," he says. "I wondered about little Terry Gibson when I first arrived. He was out of the side and I brought him back against Arsenal in January. I gave him a run of seven or eight games but he never quite managed to convince either himself or me that he was at the right club. Very often if players don't settle at Old Trafford, they just melt. It takes presence to handle the stage and Terry was one of those who never quite adjusted." Gibson went off to Wimbledon – the club who were to win the FA Cup at the end of the season.

He wasn't the only player who had to go. "My first full season saw me having to make a number of difficult decisions at both junior and senior levels. Arthur Albiston had grown up at the club and was United through and through, but he was another player topping 30 years old and we simply had too many of them in the side."

Arthur Albiston, a marvellous servant to the club, but in his thirties by the 1987/88 season.

Frank Stapleton had lost mobility and "didn't look as if he'd ever score".

By the end of Ferguson's second season at United, Kevin Moran and Graeme Hogg had joined Gibson, Stapleton and Sivebaek on the exit list. Ferguson believes he was being cruel to be kind. "I firmly believe that if you cannot honestly see first-team prospects any longer for players of their experience, it is fairer to release them," he says.

The changes he had made in training and personnel were really starting to pay dividends on the pitch. McClair was scoring more frequently than any United player since George Best, and Whiteside was looking good again up front in tandem with the Scottish player. United were still prone to drop silly points – especially away from home – but they were proving difficult to beat. The trouble was that Liverpool were having another of those Liverpool seasons, and by late January it became evident that Ferguson's main hopes lay in the cups. English clubs were still banned from Europe, making anything but a Championship win in the League largely irrelevant.

United had a good run in the League Cup, albeit against easy opposition, when they thrashed Hull in the second round and disposed of Crystal Palace and Bury in the third and fourth. The fifth round saw a return, however, to Oxford, the scene of Ferguson's first match and first defeat. The result was again 2-0 to Oxford, and United had to concentrate on the FA Cup.

The crunch match of the season, then, came as early as 20 February. The fifth round of the FA Cup saw United make the daunting trip to Highbury to face Arsenal. Things could have been worse for United at half time, but not much worse: the Gunners pulled 2-0 and cruised. But the second half saw United rally. McClair pulled back a goal, then with three minutes to go Whiteside won a penalty. McClair stepped up to notch his 21st of the season – and blasted it into the stand. With it went Ferguson's hopes for a trophy. Though United finished the season strongly, winning their last five games, and Liverpool let things slip a little, Dalglish's side ended up winning the title by nine clear points.

From second-to-bottom to second in the League wasn't bad progress for Ferguson in his first two seasons. But there was no way he could feel satisfied, because he knew that a trophy-less year at United was considered to be failure. And, on top of that, he had plenty to worry about behind the scenes at the club.

One of his major problems was the behaviour of one of his most popular players, Irishman Paul McGrath, and to a lesser degree Norman Whiteside. Both were crucial figures in the United team and both asked for transfers in the latter half of the season. The problem was one that Ferguson was already familiar with at United: alcohol.

"There's nothing wrong with having a drink," says Ferguson. "After all, I once ran a pub. But for professional footballers it has to be in moderation, at least in the run-up to matches. In the case of Norman Whiteside the problem was all to do with how he handled his injury problems. He was a truly magnificent player, but he suffered a knee injury which cost him his sharpness and pace. If it hadn't happened I am certain he would have gone on to become a truly world-class player. He was the finest in the country in terms of temperament, passing ability and footballing vision and it's refreshing to see that he's now got on with his life and become a fully qualified chiropodist. One day he could make a fine coach.

"With Paul McGrath it was a different problem. He is a deep person and he admits he has never really changed. He still seems to enjoy the social life that to me is unacceptable for a professional footballer.

"But even during the darkest days of that period, there was still a comical side to it. I will never forget the week Paul and Norman made a tour of Manchester's clubs and pubs. It was a journey charted by supporters phoning in to let me know where the two of them were and the state they were in on their merry-go-round. The important difference between them was that Paul was supposed to be in the team at the end of the week whereas Norman was out with injury. On the Saturday, Paul refused to play, saying he wasn't fit enough – which I suppose was inevitable under the circumstances. It had been quite a week and it finally drained all my patience. It was a situation which had eaten at my trust and confidence in professional footballers. So many people in the game refer to the need for a manager to hold the respect of his players. I consider it just as important for the players to have the respect of their manager. Therein lay the foundation for my decision to let players go for another season… "

But he was only putting off the weeding for later.

**Far left: McGrath; left: Whiteside.
Their off-field indiscretions
drained Fergie's patience.**

1987/88

Back row: Norman Whiteside, Chris Turner, Paul McGrath, Viv Anderson, Billy Garton, Graeme Hogg, Liam O'Brien, Gary Walsh, John Sivebaek.
Middle row: Nicky Wood, Brian Whitehouse, Jim McGregor, Joe Brown, Archie Knox, Eric Harrison, Norman Davies, Jimmy Curran, Terry Gibson.
Back row: Gordon Strachan, Peter Davenport, Mike Duxbury, Brian McClair, Kevin Moran, Alex Ferguson, Bryan Robson, Remi Moses, Colin Gibson, Arthur Albiston, Jesper Olsen.

Football League Division One

Aug 15	(a)	South'ton	D	2-2	Whiteside 2
Aug 19	(h)	Arsenal	D	0-0	
Aug 22	(h)	Watford	W	2-0	McGrath, McClair
Aug 29	(a)	Charlton A	W	3-1	McClair, Robson, McGrath
Aug 31	(h)	Chelsea	W	3-1	McClair, Strachan, Whiteside
Sep 5	(a)	Coventry	D	0-0	
Sep 12	(h)	Newcastle U	D	2-2	Olsen, McClair
Sep 19	(a)	Everton	L	1-2	Whiteside
Sep 26	(h)	Tottenham	W	1-0	McClair
Oct 3	(a)	Luton T	D	1-1	McClair
Oct 10	(a)	Sheffield W	W	4-2	Robson, McClair 2, Blackmore
Oct 17	(h)	Norwich C	W	2-1	Davenport, Robson
Oct 25	(a)	West Ham	D	1-1	Gibson
Oct 31	(h)	Notts Forest	D	2-2	Robson, Whiteside
Nov 15	(h)	Liverpool	D	1-1	Whiteside
Nov 21	(a)	Wimbledon	L	1-2	Blackmore
Dec 5	(a)	QPR	W	2-0	Davenport, Robson
Dec 12	(h)	Oxford U	W	3-1	Strachan 2, Olsen
Dec 19	(a)	Portsmouth	W	2-1	Robson, McClair
Dec 26	(a)	Newcastle U	L	0-1	
Dec 28	(h)	Everton	W	2-1	McClair 2
Jan 1	(h)	Charlton A	D	0-0	
Jan 2	(a)	Watford	W	1-0	McClair
Jan 16	(h)	South'ton	L	0-2	
Jan 24	(a)	Arsenal	W	2-1	Strachan, McClair
Feb 6	(h)	Coventry C	W	1-0	O'Brien
Feb 10	(a)	Derby Co	W	2-1	Whiteside, Strachan
Feb 13	(a)	Chelsea	W	2-1	Bruce, O'Brien
Feb 23	(a)	Tottenham	D	1-1	McClair
Mar 5	(a)	Norwich C	L	0-1	
Mar 12	(h)	Sheff Wed	W	4-1	Blackmore, McClair 2, Davenport
Mar 19	(a)	Notts Forest	D	0-0	
Mar 26	(h)	West Ham	W	3-1	Strachan, Anderson, Robson
Apr 2	(h)	Derby Co	W	4-1	McClair 3, Gibson
Apr 4	(a)	Liverpool	D	3-3	Robson 2, Strachan
Apr 12	(h)	Luton T	W	3-0	McClair, Robson, Davenport
Apr 30	(h)	QPR	W	2-1	Bruce, Parker
May 2	(a)	Oxford U	W	2-0	Anderson, Strachan
May 7	(h)	Portsmouth	W	4-1	McClair 2, Davenport, Robson
May 9	(h)	Wimbledon	W	2-1	McClair 2

Final League position: second in Division One

FA Cup
3rd Round

Jan 10	(a)	Ipswich T	W	2-1	D'Avray, Anderson

4th Round

Jan 30	(h)	Chelsea	W	2-0	Whiteside, McClair

5th Round

Feb 20	(a)	Arsenal	L	1-2	McClair

The Boss

No one could deny that Manchester United Football Club has changed beyond recognition since Alex Ferguson walked through the Old Trafford doors for the first time in November 1986. But a quick glance at the overflowing trophy cabinet only tells half the tale, for it's not just out on the pitch where things have been transformed. It was only after he had overhauled the entire club – from the youth policy to the state of the pitch, from the morale of the laundry ladies to the morale of the players – that the foundations were strong enough to launch a sustained accumulation of silverware.

"When I first came here I kept saying to myself: 'Why hasn't this club won the league for so long?'," reflects Ferguson. "And then for a long time I tried to analyse it, looking through the records season by season, checking the manager at the time and the players he had. But it was a waste of time. The only thing that matters is what you do and what the future's going to be. Once you start focusing on the proper issues you can lift the club that way.

"There are periods when I've tried to achieve things which aren't visible. I am talking about the organisation of the club within, the youth scouting and coaching, the training patterns and the behaviour of the players. They were things that were never going to be quickly appreciated or understood, because what matters at our club is winning matches and with the style and a panache that has made people so proud to support us."

The rebuilding of the club began as soon as Ferguson arrived, and no stone went unturned. He went out of his way to involve everyone who worked at the club and to make them aware of their importance. Teddy Scott, his trainer at Aberdeen, says: "He cares about people. Not only the players but the office staff and the cleaners." And it rubbed off. Ferguson quickly won over the staff, from the chairman and directors to the laundry ladies with whom he regularly chats over a cup of tea in the mornings. He tried to instil a feeling of order and pride. And, of course, when something was wrong he fixed it.

The state of the Old Trafford pitch had been a problem for years – by the end of each season it was almost bare and in winter it was bone hard. Ferguson promptly installed a new groundsman. He deemed the dressing rooms not up to scratch for a club of such stature and ordered new ones to be built. He completely transformed the way the players prepared for and travelled to matches. He changed their diet and pre-match meals. "If you let him, Steve Bruce would probably opt for a big steak with French fries and onions followed by sago pudding," he once said. He banned gambling. This was in response to his "experience with Glasgow Rangers, where it was not unknown for players to lose thousands of pounds – hardly conducive to team spirit!" He felt the training wasn't up to scratch, so he and Archie Knox changed it beyond all recognition. He wasn't intimidated by the size of the club or the size of the task. He was going to do it his way.

Jesper Olsen recalls: "Under Ron Atkinson it had been much more easy-going. Alex Ferguson came in and the training became much better organised. He was much more disciplined, we had strict guidelines on how we were to behave and it was drummed into us that we were representing Manchester United at all times. He knew what he wanted and he knew how to get there. He was given time to just get on with it, and it took time, but now you just have to look at what he's achieved."

David Meek, the former football correspondent for the *Manchester Evening News* who became closer to Ferguson than any other journalist, says: "Alex Ferguson is the first manager of the club to be completely at ease with an understanding of the job since Sir Matt Busby. He's struck a balance which others have failed to find. It's a big job, it's very demanding, and it's partly about projecting the biggest club in Britain.

"It's very easy to become distracted and neglect the team. It's also easy just to concentrate on the football side and ignore the other aspects of the club. Ferguson has struck the right balance and this is the most important element he's brought to the job – apart from the obvious, such as being a good judge of players and tactics, and a good motivator.

"He had great confidence in himself in his early years, even though he wasn't successful in terms of winning the championship. He has always planned ahead and built for the future. There was some discontent in 1990 amongst the supporters, but the board of directors stuck by him as they knew he was laying down the foundations – particularly in terms of the youth work. There was no chance of him being sacked."

Indeed, after United had won the FA Cup in 1990, United Chairman Martin Edwards told the press: "Time alone will tell. But I am sure that Alex Ferguson will lead us to even greater success. The fruits of his labours in rebuilding a vigorous youth policy, completely overhauling our scouting system and instilling a feeling of pride in everyone who wears a United shirt, will be clear for all to see before very long."

Under Ferguson, the players have never been under any illusions about the role of a Manchester United

player. He has built in time after training on Friday afternoons for the players to sign autographs, photos and balls and – as Norman Whiteside and Paul McGrath found out – he will not tolerate any indiscipline.

"He shouts a lot but his bark is much worse than his bite," says Bryan Robson, "although he frightens the young lads to death." And Steve Bruce adds: "He's mellowed a lot but he's still got this driving ambition to win. That will be with him no matter how many trophies he wins."

"That's the only way you can manage this club," insists Ferguson as he looks forward to a new challenge in 1996/97. "We must forget the wonderful days of last season. We'll take a moment to sit down and reflect and say 'Yeah, great'; but then we'll sit down and work out how to do even better. I'll go through the games and the reports I've made and assess them to see if there are certain trends we can improve on. For example, the goals we've scored and where the balance of goals is coming from. Last season we won a lot of games 1-0, and it takes an incredible amount of concentration to win a game 1-0. It's an achievement that we are capable of winning games that way, but we must be capable of winning games by more goals. If we had more of a killer touch – and it's only in certain periods during my time here that we've had that – then it would be much easier for us. So we must work on that."

"You never rest here. That's the hard part, but it's why a lot of people in the game would love to manage this club – at least they would for five or 10 minutes until they realised what a full day's work here entailed. There's always something to do, the job just gets bigger and bigger."

Archie Knox once said of Ferguson: "No matter what game he's involved in – a game of cards or anything – he wants to win, and he imposes that will on other people." At Manchester United he's imposed that will on the biggest football club in Britain, some would say the world. It was a battle. But it was a battle which, as usual, he won.

**Respected by the players, revered
by the fans: Alex is the Boss.**

Slow

1988/89

Above left: Hughesie was glad to come home;
Strachan went to Leeds United. Above centre:
Leighton joined United and Ferguson (above
right) resolved to end Liverpool's domination of
English football.

progress

It was now 22 years since Manchester United had won the League Championship, and the pressure cooker was starting to hiss. Ferguson had been at the club nearly two years and he hadn't won a trophy. The mood was upbeat at the start of the season, however, especially as the manager's pruning had earned him some extra cash enabling him to buy new players. He signed goalkeeper Jim Leighton, who had served him so well at Aberdeen, for £450,000 and, to the delight of the Old Trafford faithful, took his summer spending to £2 million by bringing Mark 'Sparky' Hughes home from exile in Spain.

Left: little Russell Beardsmore sparkled against Liverpool.
Right: "Gordon Strachan's move to Leeds triggered him back to life."

Ferguson had tried to buy Hughes the previous season but was turned down by Barcelona manager Terry Venables. This time he got his man, even though the asking price sneaked up from £1 million to £1.6 million thanks to the involvement of a transfer agent. "You cannot let the fans down after all the expectation and so we smiled and paid up," says Ferguson. Although the release of a number of players had led to a lack of strength in depth, Ferguson's jigsaw was starting to take shape and expectations were high. "We certainly approached the season in optimistic mood," he says.

The season started badly for United. A home draw with QPR was followed by defeat at Liverpool. Confidence was momentarily restored by three successive wins, but this was then followed by a run of nine games without a victory, which essentially took United out of the title race. Again, they had to concentrate on the cup competitions if they wanted to fill the gaping trophy cabinet. "I said to the directors quite early on that it wouldn't be our year for the championship. We were too erratic and selling players to raise money towards buying Sparky Hughes had left us thin on the ground when injuries struck," says Ferguson.

One chink of league light did appear on New Year's Day when United faced champions Liverpool at home. With youngsters Lee Martin and Russell Beardsmore in the side, United had a frail look about them at the beginning of the match. But Beardsmore was in sparkling form, scoring a goal and making two others, for McClair and Hughes. United ran out 3-1 winners, leaving Liverpool feeling like the lightweights. Ferguson remembers the match well: "It was a thrilling game, and we had torn them apart. I was so pleased until we were coming up the tunnel at the end of the game and Ronnie Moran said to me that the best team had lost. It was a typical Ronnie Moran statement, and I must admit it needled me because if there ever was a time we had annihilated them, that was it!"

United moved to sixth position and won four out of the next five matches, but then only managed to win three further matches in March, April and May. They had finished in 11th place again.

And so it was all down to the knock-out competitions. The League Cup campaign soon after it had started, in November, amid great controversy. After Wimbledon had bundled United out of the competition 2-1 at Plough Lane there was a fearsome fracas in the players' tunnel. "All hell was let loose in the tunnel," Ferguson remembers of the incident. "Players were pulling each other about, and Viv (Anderson) was lying on the floor, unconscious." An FA inquiry found that John Fashanu had hit Anderson, who had "directed insulting and improper comments" at the Wimbledon player. The result of the investigation was that Fashanu was banned for three games and fined £2,000 while Anderson was suspended for one game and fined £750. Ferguson is still angry about the outcome. "I asked Viv to press charges with the police because I don't think that kind of situation should be tolerated," he says. "The FA inquiry was a complete whitewash. John Fashanu defended himself and I'll never forget his magic line when he asked the disciplinary committee: 'Look, would a Dr Barnardo's boy do something like that?'"

Whatever the result of the inquiry, the result of the match meant that United had to pin all their hopes for the season on an FA Cup run. With an injury list that wouldn't have looked out of place in a field hospital, the Cup looked a long shot when the competition kicked off in January. United fought a mammoth tie with QPR, winning 3-0 in the second replay. They drubbed Oxford 4-0 in the fourth round, and knocked out Bournemouth, at the second attempt, in the fifth. Throughout the run, Ferguson had to rely on the help of a group of youngsters, mainly enlisted from the youth team, who rallied to the cause. Lee Sharpe, Lee Martin, Tony Gill, Russell Beardsmore, Deiniol Graham, David Wilson and Mark Robins all made names for themselves and gave their manager something to feel proud of. The first brood of Fergie's Fledglings had been hatched.

The quarter final against Nottingham Forest at Old Trafford, however, was a complete let down for United fans. One player in particular who failed to perform was Gordon Strachan, who put in a performance that disappointed Ferguson so much it prompted him to sell the player. "I am sure there are many people who would argue Strachan's transfer to Leeds United was in fact the biggest mistake of my career," he says of the transfer. "But I can honestly say allowing Gordon to move on was the right thing to do. There would have been no point keeping Strachan. Basically, he had run out of steam for Manchester United and to have kept him would have been a waste of time for both us and him. In my view he had not been performing for us to the standard expected of any Manchester United player, and compared to the player I knew of old, he was only a shadow of his former self."

"Matters came to a head when we were knocked out of the FA Cup by Forest. I had gone out of my way to build him up for that match, hammering home the message that the wee man was back on form and that he was the guy to take us to Wembley." Ron Atkinson wanted Strachan for Sheffield Wednesday but Ferguson had promised Leeds first refusal. "The move to Leeds triggered him back to life and the kind of form he had not shown in Manchester for some time," he says. Strachan was on his way to Leeds within hours of the final whistle. The sale was soon to have major repercussions for Ferguson and United.

Still, United were unfortunate not to make the semis. "You need luck in the FA Cup and we didn't get it against Forest," says Ferguson. "I didn't think we deserved to go out. I believe we scored a good goal which photographs later showed should have been allowed to stand. Paul McGrath put in a header which Brian McClair, in my view, forced over the line."

But there were some positive effects to be gleaned from the experience. "That defeat became a watershed in the affairs of Manchester United. I had to take stock, and my conclusion was that I'd had enough of it. Maybe Ronnie Moran's comment after the Liverpool match was still lurking around in my head, because that was the moment I decided I wasn't going to accept Liverpool's domination of English football any longer. I resolved that I had to change everything round and gather a squad capable of winning the league. I just knew I had to go for it. I realised it was all about beating fellow Scots Kenny Dalglish and George Graham, and I had this gut feeling that if I didn't have a go I wasn't going to make it as a soccer boss this side of the border."

1988/89

Back row: Viv Anderson, Neil Webb, Mike Duxbury, Billy Garton, Lee Sharpe, Mike Phelan, Lee Martin, Mal Donaghy, Steve Bruce.
Middle row: Jim McGregor, Archie Knox, Guiliana Maiorana, Gary Walsh, Jim Leighton, David Wilson, Russell Beardsmore, Norman Davies.
Back row: Mark Robins, Tony Gill, Colin Gibson, Bryan Robson, Alex Ferguson, Brian McClair, Mark Hughes, Clayton Blackmore, Ralph Milne.

Football League Division One

Date		Opponent	Res	Score	Scorers
Aug 27	(h)	QPR	D	0-0	
Sep 3	(a)	Liverpool	L	0-1	
Sep 10	(h)	Middlesbro	W	1-0	Robson
Sep 17	(a)	Luton T	W	2-0	Davenport, Robson
Sep 24	(h)	West Ham	W	2-0	Davenport, Hughes
Oct 1	(a)	Tottenham	D	2-2	Hughes, McClair
Oct 22	(a)	Wimbledon	D	1-1	Hughes
Oct 26	(h)	Norwich C	L	1-2	Hughes
Oct 30	(a)	Everton	D	1-1	Hughes
Nov 5	(h)	Aston Villa	D	1-1	Bruce
Nov 12	(a)	Derby Co	D	2-2	Hughes, McClair
Nov 19	(h)	South'ton	D	2-2	Robson, Hughes
Nov 23	(h)	Sheff Wed	D	1-1	Hughes
Nov 27	(a)	Newcastle U	D	0-0	
Dec 3	(h)	Charlton A	W	3-0	Milne, McClair, Hughes
Dec 10	(a)	Coventry C	L	0-1	
Dec 17	(a)	Arsenal	L	1-2	Hughes
Dec 26	(h)	Notts Forest	W	2-0	Milne, Hughes
Jan 1	(h)	Llverpool	W	3-1	McClair, Hughes, Beardsmore
Jan 2	(a)	Middlesbro	L	0-1	
Jan 14	(h)	Milwall	W	3-0	Blackmore, Gill, Hughes
Jan 21	(a)	West Ham	W	3-1	Strachan, Martin, McClair
Feb 5	(h)	Tottenham	W	1-0	McClair
Feb 11	(a)	Sheff Wed	W	2-0	McClair 2
Feb 25	(a)	Norwich C	L	1-2	McGrath
Mar 12	(a)	Aston Villa	D	0-0	
Mar 25	(h)	Luton T	W	2-0	Milne, Blackmore
Mar 27	(a)	Notts Forest	L	0-2	
Apr 2	(h)	Arsenal	D	1-1	Adams
Apr 8	(a)	Milwall	D	0-0	
Apr 15	(h)	Derby Co	L	0-2	
Apr 22	(a)	Charlton A	L	0-1	
Apr 29	(a)	Coventry C	L	0-1	
May 2	(h)	Wimbledon	W	1-0	McClair
May 6	(a)	South'ton	L	1-2	Beardsmore
May 8	(a)	QPR	L	2-3	Bruce, Blackmore
May 10	(h)	Everton	L	1-2	Hughes
May 13	(h)	Newcastle U	W	2-0	McClair, Robson

Final League position: 11th in Division One

FA Cup

Round	Date		Opponent	Res	Score	Scorers
3rd Round	Jan 7	(h)	QPR	D	0-0	
Replay	Jan 11	(a)	QPR	D	2-2	Gill, Graham
2nd Replay	Jan 23	(h)	QPR	W	3-0	McClair 2, Robson
4th Round	Jan 28	(h)	Oxford U	W	4-0	Hughes, Bruce, Phillips, Robson
5th Round	Feb 18	(a)	Bour'mouth	D	1-1	Hughes
Replay	Feb 22	(h)	Bour'mouth	W	1-0	McClair
6th Round	Mar 18	(h)	Notts Forest	L	0-1	

The early

transfers

In Alex Ferguson's first six months in charge at United he was linked with 104 players. The papers, it seemed, had no shortage of thoughts on who he should be buying. Ferguson, as ever, had his own ideas.

"One of the first players I had in mind was John Barnes," he says, "and our failure to get him from Watford is still a bone of contention. Graham Taylor, the Watford manager, phoned me to say that Barnes was becoming available. I had not seen him play myself and so I spoke to our chief scout, Tony Collins. The opinion of the scouting department was that Barnes was up and down, not terribly consistent.

"Unfortunately, I never got any strong indication from my scouts that they thought he was a player we should sign. A manager needs a chief scout who is prepared to commit himself with a firm decision for or against. I'm afraid Tony, maybe too much of the old school, was too cautious for me. The result was that we lost John Barnes to Liverpool and have since paid for it more than once. He would have been a wonderful player for Manchester United.

"We came to the end of the season (1987/88) and I was still looking for players. The newspapers were not short of suggestions as usual, though in my opinion the reporter who writes this rubbish doesn't know if the ball is pumped or stuffed."

It was at this time that Ferguson first became interested in a certain Middlesbrough defender by the name of Gary Pallister. Pallister was available for £600,000 but again chief scout Collins was cautious and the chance was missed. In 1988 Collins was replaced by Les Kershaw.

"I was also interested in Peter Beardsley," continues Ferguson, "but there is something peculiar about Newcastle. You never seem to get any joy out of them, at least not if you are Manchester United. Liam McFaul told me he wanted £3 million for Beardsley and then three weeks later they sold him to Liverpool for £1.9 million without even a phone call. I remembered then that their Chairman, Gordon McKeag, had refused to let us speak to Paul Gascoigne. We offered the same money as Tottenham but were not allowed to approach the player. You have to think that Newcastle don't like us."

Ferguson's first signings were relatively cheap: "On my arrival at United I was something of a Scrooge," he remarked. In the summer of 1987, he snapped up Viv Anderson from Arsenal for just £250,000; a player whose days at United were blighted by injury. That same summer he also bought Brian McClair from Celtic.

"I knew a lot about him from Scotland. He had made a big impression on me when I was at Aberdeen. He was a fluid player who always moved when his team had the ball. I was impressed with his running ability and, of course, his goals. When I came to United I knew his contract was coming up for renewal so we worked hard to get him." McClair went on to make more than 400 appearances and score more than 100 goals for the club.

The next major signing was central defender Steve Bruce in December 1987 who moved from Norwich for £800,000. "I had my eye on him for some time. I always thought of him as a player born out of sheer enthusiasm which he also generated in his team. For his height he attacked the ball well in the air and he had fair pace. I considered him a more than capable deputy for McGrath. Most importantly, though, I needed

Opposite page: United's failure to sign John Barnes infuriated Fergie. Moves for Beardsley (right) and Gascoigne (far right) were blocked.

someone to play every week and I was never disappointed on that score. He never let the club down. He cost me less than a million, but in many ways he has been our most priceless investment."

Ferguson was losing his shyness in the transfer market. "The credit for bringing Lee Sharpe to our notice was not down to a scout – the initial tip came from a retired journalist, Len Noad. I went down to see Sharpe in his fifth game for Torquay against Colchester. I wore a bonnet and scarf and sat in the back of the stand. But after about five minutes I was asked for my autograph, so obviously I would never make a spy!"

"We left 10 minutes early and went back to the car to assess him. We agreed that though he was just 17, he had a good physique, pace, and was good in the air. He had vision, awareness and it was clear when he was being man-marked that he was tough. We wanted him, and knew that if we delayed there was a good chance that the Torquay manager Cyril Knowles would be in touch with his old club, Spurs. So we went back to the club, and took Cyril for a run in the car until he had agreed to let us have Lee."

Next up was Jim Leighton who signed from Fergie's old club Aberdeen in the summer of 1988 for £450,000 ("he had served me brilliantly at Aberdeen"), followed swiftly by the return of Hughes, the prodigal son. "My own feeling is that Mark Hughes should never have been allowed to leave in the first place, but it is obviously unfair of me to criticise because I wasn't the manager at the time and I don't know all the facts. He's all blood and thunder, but there's no malice at all in that man. It was that competitive streak in him that made me pursue the return of Hughes virtually from my first weeks in the job." In the summer of 1989, Fergie got him for £1.6 million from Barcelona (via a loan spell at Bayern Munich).

A year later Neil Webb signed from Nottingham Forest despite Brian Clough's unwillingness ("I drove to the City Ground and asked to speak to Brian, the secretary came back and said he wasn't in... despite the fact that his car was parked outside"). Webb eventually played 130 games for United, but never lived up to his scoring potential with just 11 goals, well short of his Forest record well below what Fergie hoped for. An horrific Achilles tendon injury, sustained in a 1990 World Cup qualifier while playing for England, effectively put paid to his United career.

Mike Phelan arrived from Norwich for £750,000 in 1989, although Paul Ince had been Ferguson's first choice... but Incey's time would come. In the meantime the search for a central defender to partner Steve Bruce intensified. Terms were agreed with Swedish international Glenn Hysen after a meeting at Old Trafford, but the fee was pushed up by Fiorentina and Liverpool slipped in to buy him while United hesitated. All of which made Fergie even more determined to get Gary Pallister, Middlesbrough and England defender. Boro drove a hard bargain; they weren't prepared to budge from their asking price of £2.3 million and it took Ferguson six hours to persuade the board of directors to part with the cash, then a British record fee for a defender.

"We had to develop his body to make certain he was physically capable of handling the roughest and

toughest in the league. So we put him on a routine of weight training to increase his upper body strength. He is now as strong as a bull and has extra stamina that was missing before"

Danny Wallace was signed for £1.2 million from Southampton in September 1989 while Fergie pondered over whether Lee Sharpe would eventually become a left back or left winger. But the player he really wanted was still Paul Ince. He'd missed out earlier when West Ham had been changing managers, but in September 1989 he finally got his man – although it was his "most traumatic signing".

"The first difficulty arose when Paul was persuaded to wear a United shirt for a picture in one of the newspapers before he had actually signed for us. It caused us embarrassment because at that point we had not even spoken to the player."

Eventually Ince did go for talks with United and the deal went well – until, that is, he had a medical which revealed he had a pelvic problem. The transfer looked like falling through completely until it was agreed United would pay just £500,000 up front with another £1 million conditional on appearances. The deal was finally struck on 13 September 1989.

"I consider that I have done well in my spending," says Ferguson, "but I don't like this idea of Money-bags Fergie at all, particularly as I have always worked hard at establishing a successful youth policy. I believe the fans who make us the best supported club in the country expect at least one new player every season so I am sure my financial strategy has been far from extravagant. I refute the idea that Alex Ferguson has bought fecklessly."

Before United won the FA Cup in 1990 (ironically thanks to a replay goal by a product of the youth team, left back Lee Martin), Ferguson had spent more than £12 million on players and got no return. Despite a couple of disappointments, he had signed the backbone of the team (Bruce, Pallister, Ince, Hughes and Irwin – bought from Oldham after the 1990 Cup win) that would eventually break United's 26-year league hoodoo.

Wem

1989/90

bley bound

If the Old Trafford pressure cooker was hissing a year before, at the beginning of season 1989/90 it was ready to explode. United desperately needed a trophy to maintain any sort of respect at all, and Ferguson knew that if he didn't deliver one this time round, his head would be on the block and his reputation in tatters.

Michael Knighton juggled but couldn't deliver.

Nevertheless, there was a mood of optimism about the club on 19 August as United faced Arsenal at Old Trafford in the first match of the season. For one thing, Ferguson had splashed out £2.25 million on two highly-rated midfielders, England international Neil Webb from Nottingham Forest and Mike Phelan from Norwich City.

Another move that had helped lift the 47,000 crowd were the ball-juggling antics of a new saviour, businessman Michael Knighton, who'd just bought a majority shareholding in United. He announced the fact he was prepared to pump £10 million into the club, by running onto the pitch before the game dressed in full United strip.

"On the morning of the match, the chairman asked me to come and see him. He explained he had sold the club to Knighton who had offered to build a new Stretford End stand. I was quite surprised, though of course I knew about the background saga," says Ferguson of the affair. "Knighton was very pleasant and he assured me that I would get his total backing and that things would carry on more or less as before. No one will forget that first day when Michael went out on the pitch, dressed in a United strip. I tried to talk him out of it. I told him the press would crucify him, but he ignored all advice because he genuinely wanted to show he was one of the real supporters. It was done with the best of intentions but the aftermath was something we could have done without."

It seemed to inspire the players though. Within two minutes of the game, Steve Bruce had opened United's account for the season. McClair and Hughes added two more before Webb, who'd been running the show, added a fourth with 10 minutes to go. The final score was 4-1 and the situation at United suddenly started to look a bit more healthy.

It didn't last. United lost three of their next four matches, and Knighton wasn't able to come up with enough money to back his bid, and had to resign. "He came in and out of the club but had little impact because the chemistry was not right," says Ferguson, diplomatically. "He was always mannerly and supportive but his resignation was probably best under the circumstances. There was always a strain."

Knighton's departure didn't stop Ferguson from spending money. Three games into the season he lashed out £2.3 million on Middlesbrough's England international defender Gary Pallister. In mid September he paid £2 million to secure the talents of midfielder Paul Ince, and, after Neil Webb had been struck down with a long-term Achilles injury, £1.5 to Southampton for Danny Wallace. "The problem was," says Ferguson,

Mark Robins,
Fergie's lucky charm

"that my big splash in the transfer market hardly caused a ripple in terms of our League football." He can say that again. On 23 September, United went to Maine Road to face Manchester City and were thrashed 5-1. It is a result United fans are still reminded of by their City counterparts. "I felt for the fans after we lost at City," says Ferguson. "What could they say when they went into work on Monday morning?" It's unlikely that the fans felt much for Ferguson. Rumblings of discontent were starting to be heard. And it certainly hit the big man hard. "The defeat was one of the worst days of my career, with cameras around the dugout as if filming an obituary, which they nearly were," he says. The match had an early kick-off, and Ferguson was back home by 3 pm. "I went straight to my bed and put my head under the pillow. My wife Cathy came in and asked what had happened. I could hardly answer. I was in total shock and completely gone."

Worse was to follow. United didn't win a game from 25 November to 10 February, and were knocked out of the League Cup by Spurs, 3-0 at Old Trafford.

Ferguson cites the lowest point of the season being a December home defeat by Crystal Palace, who earlier in the season had been beaten 9-0 by Liverpool. Ferguson had dropped Hughes to the bench, and the crowd didn't like it. "It was, without question, the lowest, most desperate point ever in all my years of management," says Ferguson. "For the first time since the day I had arrived three years before, United's crowd turned against me. I went to see Sir Matt and he said 'How are things, son?' and I said: 'Not good, the press are giving me hell.' He just said: 'Don't read the papers then.' Such simple advice, but I couldn't think of it myself and that is as good advice I'll ever get in my life."

United finished the season on the same amount of points as Palace – 48 – only five points off a rele-

gation place. Only a priceless spell of four straight wins around Easter saved them from dropping to the Second Division, which they picked up at Southampton and QPR and at home to Coventry and Aston Villa. A young teenage striker scored in each of those games (in three of them after coming off the bench), a striker Ferguson had nurtured through the youth scheme, Mark Robins.

"Robins was our lucky charm that season," says Ferguson of his fledgling. "His goals in those games were invaluable for the safety of the club – and they weren't the only ones he scored for us that season. We threw the lad in the deep end and he proved himself a natural goalscorer. Unfortunately for him, with two strikers of the calibre of Brian McClair and Mark Hughes in the team, he couldn't get a regular place in the XI. I was very relucatant eventually to let him go to Norwich City, but in the end I had to."

Another chink of light that season was the FA Cup, and Robins was to play a big part in the outcome of that competition, too. Once again the oldest knockout competition in the world looked like being Ferguson's only hope of silverware that season, which was becoming all too common a story. United were drawn in the third round away at Nottingham Forest, the team which had knocked them out of the previous Cup, at Old Trafford. "Everybody was smelling defeat for us," says Ferguson of the Forest game. "Jimmy Hill even said we looked like a beaten team in the warm-up." There was massive speculation in the press about Ferguson's future at United resting on the result of that one match. Quite simply, Ferguson's men had to win it – and go on to lift the trophy at Wembley in May – to end the speculation.

1989/90

Back row: Lee Martin, Lee Sharpe, Mike Phelan, Viv Anderson, Steve Bruce, Paul Ince, Neil Webb, Gary Pallister.
Middle row: Archie Knox, Alex Ferguson, Mike Duxbury, Jim Leighton, Mal Donaghy, Jim McGregor, Norman Davies.
Front row: Brian McClair, Clayton Blackmore, Russell Beardsmore, Bryan Robson, Danny Wallace, Mark Robins, Ralph Milne, Mark Hughes.

Football League Division One

Date		Opponent	Result	Score	Scorers
Aug 19	(h)	Arsenal	W	4-1	Bruce, Hughes, Webb, McClair
Aug 22	(a)	Crystal P	D	1-1	Robson
Aug 26	(a)	Derby Co	L	0-2	
Aug 30	(h)	Norwich C	L	0-2	
Sep 9	(a)	Everton	L	2-3	McClair, Beardsmore
Sep 16	(h)	Millwall	W	5-1	Hughes 3, Robson, Sharpe
Sep 23	(a)	Man City	L	1-5	Hughes
Oct 14	(h)	Sheff Wed	D	0-0	
Oct 21	(a)	Coventry C	W	4-1	Bruce, Hughes 2, Phelan
Oct 28	(h)	South'ton	W	2-1	McClair 2
Nov 4	(a)	Charlton A	L	0-2	
Nov 12	(h)	Notts Forest	W	1-0	Pallister
Nov 18	(a)	Luton T	W	3-1	Wallace, Blackmore, Hughes
Nov 25	(h)	Chelsea	D	0-0	
Dec 3	(a)	Arsenal	L	0-1	
Dec 9	(h)	Crystal P	L	1-2	Beardsmore
Dec 16	(h)	Tottenham	L	0-1	
Dec 23	(a)	Liverpool	D	0-0	
Dec 26	(a)	Aston Villa	L	0-3	
Dec 30	(a)	Wimbledon	D	2-2	Hughes, Robins
Jan 1	(h)	QPR	D	0-0	
Jan 13	(h)	Derby Co	L	1-2	Pallister
Jan 21	(a)	Norwich C	L	0-2	
Feb 3	(h)	Man City	D	1-1	Blackmore
Feb 10	(a)	Millwall	W	2-1	Wallace, Hughes
Feb 24	(a)	Chelsea	L	0-1	
Mar 3	(h)	Luton T	W	4-1	McClair, Hughes, Wallace, Robins
Mar 14	(h)	Everton	D	0-0	
Mar 18	(h)	Liverpool	L	1-2	Whelan
Mar 21	(a)	Sheff Wed	L	0-1	
Mar 24	(a)	South'ton	W	2-0	Gibson, Robins
Mar 31	(h)	Coventry C	W	3-0	Hughes 2, Robins
Apr 14	(a)	QPR	W	2-1	Robins, Webb
Apr 17	(h)	Aston Villa	W	2-0	Robins 2
Apr 21	(a)	Tottenham	L	1-2	Bruce
Apr 30	(h)	Wimbledon	D	0-0	
May 2	(a)	Notts Forest	L	0-4	
May 5	(h)	Charlton A	W	1-0	Pallister

Final League position: 13th in Division One

FA Cup

Round	Date		Opponent	Result	Score	Scorers
3rd Round	Jan 7	(a)	Notts Forest	W	1-0	Robins
4th Round	Jan 28	(a)	Hereford U	W	1-0	Blackmore
5th Round	Feb 18	(a)	Newcastle U	W	3-2	Robins, Wallace, McClair
Semi-Final	Apr 8		Oldham A	D	3-3	Robson, Webb, Wallace
Semi-Final Replay	Apr 11		Oldham A	W	2-1	McClair, Robins
Final	May 12		Crystal P	D	3-3	Robson, Hughes 2
Final Replay	May 17		Crystal P	W	1-0	Martin

Fergie

and the Cup

The Cup Final is one of the greatest experiences for any manager. Alex Ferguson's love affair with the FA Cup grows deeper with every Wembley appearance.

Before the 1989/90 third round FA Cup match with Nottingham Forest, the tabloid press were baying for Ferguson's blood. But inside Old Trafford the story was a little different.

"The press wanted Martin Edwards to give me a vote of confidence before the Cup-tie and they hoped he would say that if we lost, I would be sacked," remembers Fergie of the incident. Edwards refused to play the media game, but privately told Ferguson that he would not be sacked even if United were defeated. "We knew how hard Alex Ferguson was working, not only with the first team but with the A team, the B team and at youth level. He is a bit of a workaholic. We knew the tremendous effort he was putting in and felt that eventually he would be able to turn it around," says Edwards.

United could certainly have done with an easier draw. "The night the FA Cup draw was made I was slumped at home in front of the box trying to figure out the future. Then the phone rang. It was a journalist wanting my reaction to the team we had pulled out in the Cup. What did I think? 'Pass me the rope,' is what I thought. For a moment I really believed I had been cursed. We had just been beaten 2-1 at home by Steve Coppell's Palace, the crowd had virtually howled me out of the ground and I had dropped Sparky, their big hero. And, after all that, I had pulled Cloughie's lot out of the hat and at the time they were just about the best Cup team in the country. Of course, I told the journalist in question that I was feeling absolutely wonderful about it all."

He felt better after the match, though, that's for sure – a Mark Robins strike gave United a famous victory. "The fans played a significant role for us that day," recalls Fergie. "They made sure we weren't going to lose it. Then we scrambled through 1-0 on a paddy-field of a pitch at Hereford. I always remember a whistle blowing in the second half and our players all stopped while their man ran through and Jim Leighton made a terrific save to keep us in the game. And then we scored with five minutes to go. The next game was at Newcastle and there was an unbelievable atmosphere in the ground that day. When they scored the first goal, the fans were on the pitch and battering on the top of the dugout – it felt like the whole place was falling in. We got through that 3-2, and then we won 1-0 at Sheffield United. We won easily but we kept missing chances, so we were always being kept on a knife-edge. The build-up of pace and excitement around the whole club was just getting bigger and bigger. In the semi final we had two fantastic games against Oldham. We were losing 3-2 in the second period of extra time in the first game when Mark Hughes equalised and we won the replay 1-0. That run remains with me all the time – you don't forget the excitement the FA Cup can generate."

In the other semi final, Crystal Palace pulled off a surprise defeat of Liverpool. On 12 May, United and Palace served up one of the classic Wembley finals of all time. With United 2-1 up and 20 minutes on the clock, Ian Wright came off the bench. Within three minutes he had equalised, then two minutes into extra time he put Palace ahead. United poured forward and eventually, miraculously, Mark Hughes took the Cup to a replay – and probably saved his manager's job.

In the replay Ferguson made the brave but controversial decision to drop his goalkeeper. "As we were trooping off the field, I looked at Jim Leighton and I knew he was a beaten man. In the dressing room he sat with his head between his knees and it was then I knew he had to be left out of the replay. If I could have my time over again, I would not drop Jim Leighton... not because it was wrong from a football point of view, but because it wrecked his career and cost him two years of his footballing life. But the easy decision was to play him again. The hard decision won us the Cup." Lee Martin scored the only goal of a scrappy match and delivered Ferguson his first trophy at Old Trafford. The win had won Ferguson some time and respect, and had satisfied for a while the demand to fill the Old Trafford trophy cabinet.

Having tasted FA Cup Final victory at Wembley, Ferguson grew hungry for more. "Going to Wembley is special; the excitement heightens with each round of the FA Cup. I won the Scottish Cup four times with Aberdeen but you don't get any of the acceleration of excitement I've experienced with United. It's a fabulous competition, it's great and the fans love it. Because it's sudden death and you can lose a game in a second, there's a climactic feel to every game as it progresses."

Above: Alex celebrates the historic double double.
Right: *le goal*,
1996 FA Cup Final.

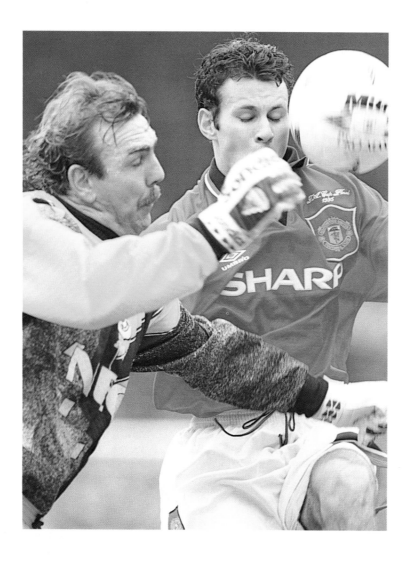

Ferguson's Cup record both north and south of the border is remarkable. Since 1982 he's not only won the Scottish Cup four times, but the FA Cup three times – as well as managing the losing finalists in 1995. So what's the secret of his Cup success? "You need winners to get through Cup-ties and we've got winners here, we always have had. People like Bruce, Cantona, Hughes, Ince, McClair, Schmeichel. At Aberdeen I had Miller, McLeish, Kennedy, Simpson, Cooper, McGhee, Strachan – they're all winners. At United, once the team get through the early Cup stages, they start to smell the hot dogs because they're used to playing at Wembley.

"In the FA Cup, normally the matches are tight and intense. People say 'how can you enjoy it?' But I do; it's fantastic, it's exciting, and I think the players feel the same way. To a large extent I suppose the team is a mirror of me."

And his favourite Wembley triumph? "Oh, the last one in 1996 without a shadow of a doubt. Beating Liverpool, our great rivals, with three minutes to go – there was just no way back for them. To beat your greatest rival in the final at Wembley: you won't forget that."

When it comes to the Cup competitions there's always luck involved, but experience is bound to count – and Ferguson's had plenty of that. "I remember at Aberdeen losing one of my early League Cup Finals 3-0 against Dundee United. The game was only three minutes old when I knew I had made a mistake and picked

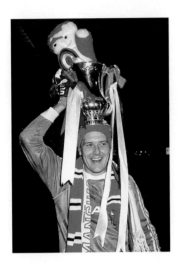

the wrong team. Looking back, I realise I had got caught up in the personal medical problem of one of the younger players, and that had completely diverted my attention. That experience, probably more than a lot of happier occasions, helped to forge my character in management terms. I suffered through the night but was up and running at eight the next morning, and I shook the hand of each one of the players to say thank you for getting the team to the Cup Final."

Ferguson's first ever taste of Cup drama was as a player with Dunfermline, but it was one of bitter disappointment. Not only did his side lose 3-2 but he was dropped for the match, despite being the club's leading scorer at the time. It was an experience that, however devastating, stood him in good stead for the future. Jim Leighton wasn't the only big-name player Ferguson has dropped for an FA Cup Final. In 1994 he had to tell Bryan Robson he was leaving him out of the starting line-up for the FA Cup Final against Chelsea, but it was a decision justified by the 4-0 mauling of Glenn Hoddle's side – which came despite the even-stevens first half. "As we approached the Cup Final, if there was any nervousness or anxiety in the dressing room it was because we were all filled with the desire to do that extra special something in Sir Matt Busby's memory. All his family were there at Wembley and I think they took pride in the way the team performed that day. It was terribly disappointing to lose to Everton the following year, but it is a game we would have won if we'd won the league – these things happen in Cup football. We were in total control in the second half, but Brian McClair was unlucky with a header which hit the bar and Neville Southall played the way he hadn't played for years – the second time in a week we ran into a keeper who was having an inspired day."

A year later in 1996, it was all forgotten when Eric Cantona's delightful volley hit the back of the Wembley net and history was made. It was Ferguson's third FA Cup win, and he and United had won the first ever double double in the history of English football. The game might not have looked pretty, but victory still tasted sweet.

"Wembley can be such a slow pitch and it produces games like that. The Cup Final needs an early goal but in 1996 against Liverpool it didn't come and both teams got caught up in the possession game. Our attitude is always to win and always to entertain – it always has been. The point with Liverpool's system is that it's hard to get the ball off them. When we did, it was very difficult for us to then get it forward to Cantona. The goal, however, was something else. It took such balance, composure and accuracy. When you see it again it's such a great goal, incredible."

Incredible. In fact, just like Ferguson's Cup record. And you get the feeling there might just be a few more tales to tell in years to come, and you can be damn sure there'll be a glint in his eye when he's telling them.

1990/91

to Europe

United's Cup win meant that, despite their poor League form, they had earned themselves a place in Europe. 1990/91 was the season UEFA allowed English clubs back into the continental competitions after five post-Heysel years in the wilderness. The European Cup Winners' Cup

Denis Irwin: great buy, great defender.

The manager had further strengthened his squad in the summer by signing an Irish full back from Oldham who had impressed him in the previous season's FA Cup semi final. Denis Irwin was to prove something of a bargain at £625,000.

Once again, however, as the season progressed, United were too inconsistent to make much of a mark in the League. The season was dominated by George Graham's parsimonious Arsenal side, against whom it was almost impossible to score. United faced the Gunners at Old Trafford on 20 October in a match that was to have long-lasting consequences. Arsenal won the encounter 1-0, as was their wont. But it was the fracas on the pitch, which involved every player bar David Seaman and followed a late and dangerous tackle by Anders Limpar on Irwin, that caught the press's attention the next day. Ferguson now tries to play the whole thing down: "Some called it a brawl; I thought it was more handbags at dawn," he says. Nevertheless the FA saw fit to dock Arsenal two points and United one point. Ferguson himself fined Ince, McClair and Irwin for their role in the affair, a move he now regrets. "I did it because I felt the club and myself were under pressure and people were expecting some positive action," he says.

Five weeks after the Battle of Old Trafford, United went to Highbury to play Arsenal in the Rumbelows Cup. Lee Sharpe was in devastating form and scored a hat-trick in an amazing 6-2 win. "To score six at Highbury was special, but the main significance was that it signalled the arrival of a remarkable talent in the shape of Lee Sharpe, who had battled back from injury problems. He revealed exciting pace in a team I picked specifically to beat Arsenal after losing to them at Old Trafford," says Ferguson. United had beaten Halifax and Liverpool to get to that point in the competition. They were to go all the way to the final, after disposing of Southampton (after a replay) and Leeds (after a two-legged semi final). In the second leg at Elland Road, Sharpe was again the hero, scoring the only goal of the match to send United to Wembley for the second year running. It was a tough match and Ferguson was happy to see the back of his Yorkshire rivals. "There is a lot of aggression in the Leeds game, and they have the most intimidating support in football," he says.

United arrived at the final against Ron Atkinson's Second Division outfit Sheffield Wednesday at Wembley on 21 April, tired after a European match in mid-week. "Our soft approach resulted in our not keeping possession enough," says Ferguson of the match. "There was an element of 'Let's just give it to Sharpey and he'll win it for us.' He was in hot form but, although he is a good player, one man doesn't do it on his own at Wembley. They scored just before half time and when that happens to you in a Cup Final you know you have a big job on your hands." Too big, in fact. John Sheridan's goal was enough to take the trophy to Sheffield, and United, having been knocked out of the FA Cup by Norwich and trailing Arsenal by a huge total in the League, had to concentrate on the European Cup Winners' Cup.

The last thing Ferguson needed the next morning was a bombshell. He was at his desk, wondering where everything had gone wrong, when he received a phone call from Rangers manager Walter Smith who told him he'd put in an offer for his assistant, Archie Knox. "I was shocked to say the least, but Archie was keen to accept and I realised they'd given him a huge financial offer. It was all terribly upsetting, but I take absolutely nothing away from Archie's contribution. He had worked himself into the ground for us. He was always a beast for work and he had been important not just at first-team level, but in what he had done to create our School of Excellence and set up the schoolboy operation with Brian Kidd."

Knox's decision was harder to bear as it came just two days before the second leg of United's European Cup Winners' Cup semi final against Legia Warsaw. United had progressed to that stage of the competition like a bunch of European veterans – instead of a team who, for the most part, were fighting their first campaign on the continent. They had easily beaten Pesci Munkas and Wrexham home and away in the first two rounds before stumbling in the first leg against Montpellier by drawing 1-1 at Old Trafford. To their credit United took the game to the French in Montpellier, and returned to Manchester with a 2-0 win and a place in the semi final under their belts. "It was a really top performance," says Ferguson. "Many of the pundits, and perhaps even some of our followers, had written us off. But our travelling support was wonderful and created a European night to savour." United desperately wanted to avoid Barcelona and Juventus in the semi final, and luck was with them in the draw. Legia Warsaw seemed a much easier task. United travelled to Warsaw and, despite going a goal down early on, fought back to win 3-1. They finished off the Poles by drawing the return 1-1 at Old Trafford.

The scene was set for the final in Rotterdam against one of the best teams in Europe, Johan Cruyff's Barcelona. "As we approached the final the first challenge I had to meet was to get the selection and

McClair strikes against Montpellier.

Mark Hughes scores the dramatic winning goal to beat Barcelona, his former club, in the European Cup Winners' Cup Final – a precise finish from an acute angle.

tactics right. I enjoy a good managerial battle of wits and I tried to read what Cruyff would do against us. I worked out that he would play with one centre back to leave Ronald Koeman free to set things up, so we put Brian McClair on Koeman to choke his efforts and make him work hard," remembers Ferguson.

The manager played a straight 4-4-2 formation against the newly crowned Spanish Champions: "A British system which has served our clubs so well over the years, especially in European competition." Again he brought in Les Sealey for a major final, wanting "an experienced lad" in goal rather than Gary Walsh. Mark Hughes was the star of the night. Rejected by Barcelona earlier in his career, he had a score to settle. A tap-in goal on 68 minutes didn't satisfy the Welshman, but a vicious, vengeful thumper from the tightest of angles did. Koeman pulled a goal back for Barça with a trademark free-kick, had a goal disallowed, and Blackmore cleared off the line in the last few minutes, but the trophy was Manchester United's. It was their first European success since Busby won the European Cup in 1968.

United returned in triumph. The bus ride from Manchester Airport took three hours to get to the city centre as it passed through thousands of joyous fans. "The volume of people in Manchester took my breath away," says Ferguson, "particularly when I saw Man City supporters joining in the welcome home! I shall never forget the whole experience. The goals were obviously memorable, but for me the lasting impression was the atmosphere in the Feyenoord Stadium and watching the jubilation of our supporters in the pouring rain." They were going to get used to jubilation, those United fans.

Choccy congratulates Sparky on his brilliant winner against Barcelona.

1990/91

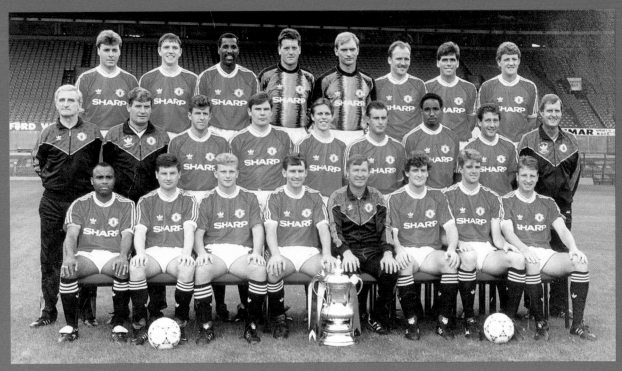

Back row: Mal Donaghy, Lee Sharpe, Viv Anderson, Les Sealey, Jim Leighton, Mike Phelan, Neil Webb, Steve Bruce.
Middle row: Jim McGregor, Archie Knox, Colin Gibson, Brian McClair, Russell Beardsmore, Clayton Blackmore, Paul Ince, Ralph Milne, Norman Davies.
Front row: Danny Wallace, Denis Irwin, Mark Robins, Brian McClair, Alex Ferguson, Mark Hughes, Gary Pallister, Lee Martin.

Football League Division One

Aug 25	(h)	Coventry C	W 2-0	Bruce, Webb
Aug 28	(a)	Leeds	D 0-0	
Sep 1	(a)	Sunderland	L 1-2	McClair
Sep 4	(a)	Luton T	W 1-0	Robins
Sep 8	(h)	QPR	W 3-1	McClair, Robins 2
Sep 16	(a)	Liverpool	L 0-4	
Sep 22	(h)	South'ton	W 3-2	McClair, Blackmore, Hughes
Sep 29	(h)	Notts Forest	L 0-1	
Oct 20	(h)	Arsenal	L 0-1	
Oct 27	(a)	Man City	D 3-3	Hughes, McClair 2
Nov 3	(h)	Crystal P	W 2-0	Webb, Wallace
Nov 10	(a)	Derby Co	D 0-0	
Nov 17	(h)	Sheffield U	W 2-0	Bruce, Hughes
Nov 25	(h)	Chelsea	L 2-3	Wallace, Hughes
Dec 1	(a)	Everton	W 1-0	Sharpe
Dec 8	(h)	Leeds U	D 1-1	Webb
Dec 15	(a)	Coventry C	D 2-2	Hughes, Wallace
Dec 22	(a)	Wimbledon	W 3-1	Bruce 2, Hughes
Dec 26	(h)	Norwich C	W 3-0	Hughes, McClair 2
Dec 29	(h)	Aston Villa	D 1-1	Bruce
Jan 1	(a)	Tottenham	W 2-1	Bruce, McClair
Jan 12	(h)	Sunderland	W 3-0	Hughes 2, McClair
Jan 19	(a)	QPR	D 1-1	Phelan
Feb 3	(h)	Liverpool	D 1-1	Bruce
Feb 26	(a)	Sheffield U	L 1-2	Blackmore
Mar 2	(h)	Everton	L 0-2	
Mar 9	(a)	Chelsea	L 2-3	Hughes, McClair
Mar 13	(a)	South'ton	D 1-1	Ince
Mar 16	(a)	Motts Forest	D 1-1	Blackmore
Mar 23	(h)	Luton T	W 4-1	Bruce 2, Robins, McClair
Mar 30	(a)	Norwich C	W 3-0	Bruce 2, Ince
Apr 2	(h)	Wimbledon	W 2-1	Bruce, McClair
Apr 6	(a)	Aston Villa	D 1-1	Sharpe
Apr 16	(h)	Derby Co	W 3-1	Blackmore, McClair, Robson
May 4	(h)	Man City	W 1-0	Giggs
May 6	(a)	Arsenal	L 1-3	Bruce
May 11	(a)	Crystal P	L 0-3	
May 20	(h)	Tottenham	D 1-1	Ince

Final League position: sixth in Division One

FA Cup

3rd Round Jan 7	(h)	QPR	W 2-1	Hughes, McClair
4th Round Jan 26	(h)	Bolton W	W 1-0	Hughes
5th Round Feb 18	(a)	Norwich C	L 1-2	McClair

European Cup Winners' Cup

1st Round (1st Leg)	Sep 19 (h)	Pecsi M	W 2-0	Blackmore, Webb
1st Round (2nd Leg)	Oct 3 (a)	Pecsi M	W 1-0	McClair
2nd Round (1st Leg)	Oct 23 (h)	Wrexham	W 3-0	McClair, Bruce, Pallister
2nd Round (2nd Leg)	Nov 7 (a)	Wrexham	W 2-0	Robins, Bruce
Quarter-Final (1st Leg)	Mar 6 (h)	Montpellier	D 1-1	McClair
Quarter-Final (2nd Leg)	Mar 19 (a)	Montpellier	W 2-0	Blackmore, Bruce
Semi-Final (1st Leg)	Apr 10 (a)	L Warsaw	W 3-1	McClair, Hughes, Bruce
Semi-Final (2nd Leg)	Apr 24 (h)	L Warsaw	D 1-1	Sharpe
Final	May 15	Barcelona	W 2-1	Hughes 2

Above left: Brian Kidd leads from the
front in pre-season training, July 1996.
Above centre: sending signals.
Above right: we won the Cup!

Kiddo

It's one of the enduring memories of United's recent successes. In celebration of

Ferguson's assistants have always been important to him. But as the United job has grown and grown, so inevitably has the importance of the role of the man at his right hand shoulder.

"Brian brings me loyalty and I depend on him," explains Ferguson. "When I am away I know that things are being done properly, that is a big comfort. He is not a shadow of me and he has his own opinions. We are always discussing the team and possible new signings, sometimes we agree and sometimes we don't. That's the way a partnership should be. With Brian I always get good feedback, I always get different opinions and, of course, I always have someone with whom to celebrate goals."

When Ferguson first arrived at United, he brought his old Aberdeen partner Archie Knox as assistant manager. "He was my first signing," says Ferguson, "he knew the importance of hard work at this level." The two had formed a rock solid partnership which had landed trophy after trophy north of the border for the Dons.

At Old Trafford, Knox immediately set about improving the training routines that so shocked Ferguson when he arrived at the club. Ferguson recalls: "I had to look at the standard of fitness at the club and I came to the conclusion that it simply wasn't good enough. There was no way you could expect the players to compete in 60 battles to the level demanded of Manchester United. Archie, who had always worked like a beat himself, took charge of fitness training and it wasn't long before we were reaping the benefits."

But before the benefits of the new regime could be truly reaped, Archie Knox dropped his bombshell. Three days before the 1991 European Cup Winners' semi final and the day after United had lost the Rumbelows Cup Final, new Rangers manager Walter Smith telephoned Ferguson to say he had asked Knox to become his assistant.

"We tried to persuade him to stay, offered him better terms, but he'd made up his mind. So when it was all agreed, I asked him when they expected him to start at Ibrox. He said 'tomorrow'. There was nothing more to say. I thanked him for what he had done for me and wished him all the best. There was no point in parting enemies. I respected the work he had done at Old Trafford and, while I didn't agree with his decision, I had to respect the offer he had received. Archie was a man who I could always trust, and that's exactly what you need in an assistant."

With the importance Ferguson attached to the role, finding a successor to the man with whom he'd worked for the best part of the last 15 years was one task he was not relishing. In the end, however, he didn't have to look far to fill the vacancy.

"Brian Kidd had been playing an increasingly important role at the club," he recalls. "He had, of course, played through the ranks at Old Trafford after joining as a schoolboy star from Collyhurst, the school attended by Nobby Stiles. His career took him to a number of clubs, but I think United was always his first and last love. He had done an excellent job with our schoolboy coaching and I eventually took him onto the permanent staff to do even more in the field of finding and signing youngsters. It was nice to have another United old boy on the staff. His enthusiasm and coaching ability shone through and so, after considering a number of possibilities, I promoted him to become Archie Knox's successor at the start of the 1991/92 season."

For Kidd the appointment came right out of the blue. "At first I didn't want it. At the time I was very content and settled in my job as Youth Development Officer. We were all sat in the coaches' office before the new season, and the Boss was organising his staff. He just said, "Kiddo, give me a hand with the first team, will you? I said to myself: 'What's going on here?' I just couldn't believe what I was hearing! I didn't really know why the Boss opted for me – I still don't – but he obviously saw something there."

Ferguson explains what it is that he saw: "Brian is dedicated and he's committed to the club. I can rest easy knowing that the training sessions are in good order and that the right training is being done. Getting the training right is crucial, especially during winter, and Kiddo is excellent at judging what is needed. He knows from his own experience how much to give them and when to rest them. That is invaluable. Kiddo has to set a programme, then we chat about it. If there is anything functional, I'll come in and do that and, if there is any coaching, I'll sometimes come in and do that too. But in the main Brian gets on with it.

Kidd has built up a great rapport with his players. It is a kind of love/hate relationship – he directs his harsh training programmes with a cheeky smile and a bucket load of banter. "He's brilliant at leading the training," says Ryan Giggs. "He studies all sorts of methods and always has new ideas. He went to

Italy, to Milan and Parma, to study their methods and came back saying all they do is shooting practice. So in the afternoons, it became a bit of a habit for a group of us to stay on and do some shooting practice. I found it really helped. I often go along to Wigan rugby league with Brian Kidd; he's always on the look-out for new training methods. He studies other sports incessantly to check out the way they operate and see if there's anything he can use for us."

And his relationship with the gaffer? Kidd explains: "I can only speak for myself, but I think we've got a great relationship. I get on very well with him as a person which I think is vital when you're working closely with someone, and he's taught me a lot about managing a football club. The Boss is a very honest and loyal man which means that everyone knows where they stand, and if he's got something to say to you he'll say it to your face, which I really appreciate in a person."

"Sometimes Alex and I argue like cat and dog – we're like an old married couple – but I think that it's sometimes healthy to have different views and opinions when you're discussing things. Also, neither of us is afraid to analyse ourselves if things aren't going well. If we need to be blamed for something, then we'll accept it – a bad result isn't necessarily the sole fault of the players."

It's a working relationship that forms the top of a huge pyramid of staff at United, a pyramid which Ferguson has ensured is re-inforced at every level. His major appointments include bringing in Jim Ryan and former United star Bryan 'Pop' Robson to develop the club's school of excellence which is now bearing such fruit.

Of all the key elements at the club, however, none is more important to his manager than Brian Kidd. "I keep my finger on the button with his assistance," Ferguson claims. "It's not a question of going into minute detail with him every day, but he helps with all the necessary dressing room feedback that I need to know. There is so much happening at this club that I have what I call my 'built-in trivia deflector' which makes sure the important issues end up planted in the brain, and the rubbish is filtered out. Kiddo, I fully appreciate, is a crucial part of the Ferguson system that runs United."

**Opposite, far left: the 1996 Premiership trophy;
left, the 1996 FA Cup.
Above: the masterminds behind them.**

Great ex

1991/92

Above left: Rumbelows Cup triumph.
Above centre: young genius.
Above right: Brucey hoists the silverware.

pectations

Alex Ferguson was feeling optimistic at the start of the 1991/92 season. He had seen his side win the Cup Winners' Cup; he had witnessed the emergence of rising teenage star Ryan Giggs; he had bought rushing Russian winger Andrei Kanchelskis, Danish international keeper Peter Schmeichel and England full-back Paul Parker. Indeed, he felt that 1991/92 would be United's season for the League Championship, and said as much before a ball was kicked. "Flushed with the success of Europe, I stuck my neck right out," he says. "Some no doubt considered I was foolish to be so bold, but I honestly thought we were ripe for a serious assault on the League Championship. It was not a matter of getting carried away, but simply a declaration of intent for the supporters of Manchester United."

**New blood: Parker (far left) and Schmeichel (left).
Opposite page: the fans wallow in Wembley victory.**

He was right about United making a serious bid for the title, all right. By Boxing Day, when they thrashed Oldham 6-3 at Boundary Park, United looked like they would run away with the race. They won eight of their first 10 matches, and 14 of their first 20. "I knew from the way we started we were going to win and that was a regular feeling around this time," he says of the mood at Old Trafford.

The New Year, however, started appallingly for United, with a disastrous 4-1 defeat at home to Queens Park Rangers. "It came as such a shock that people just had to find a reason for it, and some invented their own," says Ferguson. "The most popular theory was that the players were drunk the night before because we were celebrating at a New Year's Eve party. The other theory doing the rounds was that people had seen the players in various pubs the day before the game. That was absolute nonsense as well, because we were all together in a hotel, overnight." The truth is that United were suffering from a flu epidemic, the crowd was low due to live coverage on television and the team found it difficult to cope with a strange five o'clock kick-off – so difficult, in fact, that they were two goals down inside 10 minutes.

January was a crucial month, because it featured away fixtures against Leeds in each of the three domestic competitions – and Leeds were United's main rivals that year. "They were three absorbing games which demanded absolute concentration and energy. I know we were totally drained at the end of them and Leeds, I think, were the same," says Ferguson. The two Uniteds drew 1-1 at Elland Road in the League game. Manchester triumphed 3-1 in the Rumbelows Cup and 1-0 in the FA Cup. A bit of a hollow triumph, as it turns out. "The folly of winning both Cup-ties," explains Ferguson, "was brought home to roost towards the end of the season. I've got to say, though, that it was a period of intense commitment and great drama as we battled against the draining effect of those Cup-ties. Publicly I kept saying that we had the players to handle it, but privately I was worried because we had freed Leeds for a clear run-in for the Championship while we continued to battle on three fronts. Of the three games the one I most wanted to win was the League fixture, and of course we drew. If we had beaten Leeds we would have gone seven points clear."

The FA Cup win over Leeds saw United progress to the fourth round, where they met Southampton at the Dell. A 0-0 draw was followed by the last thing United wanted – a replay at Old Trafford. The game finished 2-2, but United lost on penalties.

The Rumbelows Cup win saw United in the semi final, a tough two-legged affair against Middlesbrough. United battled for a 0-0 draw at Ayresome, then won 2-1 at Old Trafford to set up a Wembley date with Brian Clough's Nottingham Forest. "I felt confident about beating Forest," says Ferguson. "We worked out a strategy to counter them (especially Nigel Clough and Roy Keane) and, in the main, we controlled the match very well." McClair scored the winner, the only goal of the game.

This was Manchester United's first ever League Cup Final victory, and meant that Ferguson had won two trophies that season. McClair had again scored the only goal of the game against Red Star Belgrade to bring United the Super Cup in November, making up for their early exit from the Cup Winners' Cup to Atletico Madrid. But it had also added to United's fixture jam – all through April, Ferguson's men played two games a week – and the strain was starting to show. United were scoring half the goals they had been scoring in the first half of the season, and wins were becoming few and far between. It made for one of the most thrilling Championship run-ins for years.

United faced five games in 10 days after the Wembley Final. Having jumped the first hurdle with a nervous 1-0 home win over Southampton, and limped over the second with a 1-1 draw at Luton, United faced Forest again – this time at Old Trafford. Ferguson controversially left Mark Hughes, who hadn't scored in 10 matches, on the bench. "Mark has a great many qualities, but sooner or later you have got to assess the scoring and, in particular, the centre forward's goals. When I left him out of the Forest game he'd had a run of bad form and sometimes the only way out of that is a break from the action to ease the expectation. I made him a substitute and I believe it was the best thing that could have happened to him. The crowd were chanting his name as he sat on the bench, reinforcing Mark's belief in his ability and self-respect."

Maybe they could have done with him on the pitch, as Ferguson all but admits. "We annihilated Forest," he says. "They didn't get a corner kick, but our luck seemed to be out because we lost 2-1. They grabbed a winner near the end to leave me examining our scoring. Or, more accurately, our lack of scoring." Leeds, galvanised by the recent arrival of a Frenchman called Eric Cantona, moved one point clear, but United still had a game in hand.

Two days later, United faced West Ham at Upton Park to even up the games played. Ferguson was furious at the effort West Ham put into the match, and made an outburst similar to his attack in 1995/96 on Leeds United. "I thought the West Ham performance was obscene in the sense of the almost criminal effort they put into the game," he said. The Hammers were already relegated but steamed into United, and ran out 1-0 winners. "It was a black day and a bad result for us," says Ferguson. "If I had been Billy Bonds I would have wanted to know why my players had not fought like that when their own future was at stake."

The final blow came when United lost their penultimate game 0-2, at Liverpool of all places. On the same day Leeds won 3-2 at Sheffield United to ensure the Championship. "The players gave everything but, in our hearts, I think we probably knew we had put Leeds in the driving seat," says Ferguson. But following United's failure he remained up-beat about United's trophy chances in 1992/93. "The important thing is that we must not allow ourselves to think that Manchester United's failure to win the League title since 1967 is some kind of curse on the club. We must not sink into a trough of despondency, believing that the world is against us, because that way lies defeat and the possibility of submission. The players' failure could make them better men and players of distinction. It might just be the final lesson as we work towards creating a team in the fullest meaning of the word." Having sorted out the dejection at the club, he cleared things up at home, too. "The final few weeks drained me, no question about that, and they drained my wife Cathy, too. Our house was like a morgue. She said she didn't know whether she could go through it all again but we talked that one through and from now on she's going to let me do the worrying."

Distraught players contemplate League failure.

1991/92

Back row: Brian McClair, Paul Ince, Ryan Giggs, Russell Beardsmore, Darren Ferguson.
Middle row: Jim McGregor, Andrei Kanchelskis, Steve Bruce, Jim Leighton, Peter Schmeichel, Gary Pallister, Neil Webb, Lee Sharpe, Norman Davies.
Front row: Danny Wallace, Clayton Blackmore, Paul Parker, Brian Kidd, Bryan Robson, Alex Ferguson, Lee Martin, Denis Irwin, Mark Hughes.

Football League Division One

Date		Opponent		Score	Scorers
Aug 17	(h)	Notts Co	W	2-0	Hughes, Robson
Aug 21	(a)	Aston Villa	W	1-0	Bruce
Aug 24	(a)	Everton	D	0-0	
Aug 28	(h)	Oldham A	W	1-0	McClair
Aug 31	(h)	Leeds	D	1-1	Robson
Sep 3	(a)	Wimbledon	W	2-1	Blackmore, Pallister
Sep 7	(h)	Norwich C	W	3-0	Irwin, McClair, Giggs
Sep 14	(a)	South'ton	W	1-0	Hughes
Sep 21	(h)	Luton T	W	5-0	Ince, Bruce, McClair 2, Hughes
Sep 28	(a)	Tottenham	W	2-1	Hughes, Robson
Oct 6	(h)	Liverpool	D	0-0	
Oct 19	(h)	Arsenal	D	1-1	Bruce
Oct 26	(a)	Sheff Wed	L	2-3	McClair 2
Nov 2	(h)	Sheffield U	W	2-0	Beesley, Kanchelskis
Nov 16	(a)	Man City	D	0-0	
Nov 23	(h)	West Ham	W	2-1	Giggs, Robson
Nov 30	(a)	Crystal P	W	3-1	Webb, McClair, Kanchelskis
Dec 7	(h)	Coventry C	W	4-0	Bruce, Webb, McClair, Hughes
Dec 15	(a)	Chelsea	W	3-1	Irwin, McClair, Bruce
Dec 26	(a)	Oldham A	W	6-3	Irwin 2, Kanchelskis, McClair 2, Giggs
Dec 29	(a)	Leeds U	D	1-1	Webb
Jan 1	(h)	QPR	L	1-4	McClair
Jan 11	(h)	Everton	W	1-0	Kanchelskis
Jan 18	(a)	Notts Co	D	1-1	Blackmore
Jan 22	(h)	Aston Villa	W	1-0	Hughes
Feb 1	(a)	Arsenal	D	1-1	McClair
Feb 8	(h)	Sheff Wed	D	1-1	McClair
Feb 22	(h)	Crystal P	W	2-0	Hughes 2
Feb 26	(h)	Chelsea	D	1-1	Hughes
Feb 29	(a)	Coventry C	D	0-0	
Mar 14	(a)	Sheffield U	W	2-1	McClair, Blackmore
Mar 18	(a)	Notts Forest	L	0-1	
Mar 21	(h)	Wimbledon	D	0-0	
Mar 28	(a)	QPR	D	0-0	
Mar 31	(a)	Norwich C	W	3-1	Ince 2, McClair
Apr 7	(h)	Man City	D	1-1	Giggs
Apr 16	(h)	South'ton	W	1-0	Kanchelskis
Apr 18	(a)	Luton T	D	1-1	Sharpe
Apr 20	(h)	Notts Forest	L	1-2	McClair
Apr 22	(a)	West Ham	L	0-1	
Apr 26	(a)	Liverpool	L	0-2	
May 2	(h)	Tottenham	W	3-1	McClair, Hughes 2

Final League position: second in Division One

FA Cup

3rd Round

Jan 15	(a)	Leeds U	W	1-0	Hughes

4th Round

Jan 27	(a)	South'ton	D	0-0	

Replay

Feb 5	(h)	South'ton	D	2-2	Kanchelskis, McClair

Southampton won 4-2 on penalties

European Cup Winners' Cup

1st Round (1st Leg)

Sep 18	(a)	Athinaikos	D	0-0	

1st Round (2nd Leg)

Oct 2	(h)	Athinaikos	W	2-0	Hughes, McClair

2nd Round (1st Leg)

Oct 23	(a)	A Madrid	L	0-3	

2nd round (2nd Leg)

Nov 6	(h)	A Madrid	D	1-1	

More

transfers

It's a drizzly November morning in 1992 and Alex Ferguson and Martin Edwards are at Old Trafford, running through a list of top strikers they want to sign, after their £3.5 million bid for Sheffield Wednesday's David Hirst was turned down...

"We were nattering on, shuffling though names," recalls Ferguson, "and I mentioned it was a pity we didn't get a sniff a season earlier when Cantona was first brought to this country. Then the phone rang and Martin picked it up. On the other end was Bill Fotherby, the managing director at Elland Road, who was interested in buying Denis Irwin. The timing was weird, absolutely uncanny.

"Martin, automatically knowing the answer, glanced across at me. 'No chance at all,' I reassured him. Then, in whispers and sign language, I tried to initiate a conversation about Cantona. Martin didn't get the drift, so I scribbled Eric's name on a bit of paper and eased it across the desk. Immediately Martin tuned in and suggested to Bill that the word on the grapevine was that Cantona wasn't too happy at Leeds after some backroom bust-up. Bill pleaded ignorance.

"'All the same,' said Martin, 'any chance of you selling him and we'd be interested. Need to know pretty quick, mind you, because we have the money for a striker and want to do business now. If Eric's not available, we'll go elsewhere.' Bill rang off with the promise that he would consult Howard Wilkinson. I scooted off to Coventry on business, but within an hour Leeds were back and the haggling began.

"I started on the motorway journey back and the carphone buzzed in my ear. 'We've got him,' the chairman explained. 'How much do you think?' Trying to be realistic, I said £1.6 million. 'Wrong,' he said, so I rattled off three or four more attempts. They were all far off the mark, not anywhere close. Eventually the chairman declared the true figure: £1 million. I just couldn't believe it. 'That's an absolute steal,' I said."

Alex Ferguson had just made his most important signing ever. By passing a piece of paper across a desk he'd just slipped the final piece of the jigsaw into place.

"We met Cantona at a hotel in Manchester. He came with Jean-Jacques Bertrand from the PFA in France. The chairman got his calculator out and said: 'We'll do that.' Eric and I were just having a cup of tea. Eric didn't speak much English, and I was practising my French.

"And the chairman said: 'Right, that's that, can we shake on that?'

"Jean-Jacques said: 'Yes.'

"'Eric, you haven't told Eric,' I said.

"And Jean-Jacques never even asked Eric if he was happy with it. Eric always trusts him to do the deal. But the whole thing must have taken just half an hour because I'd left Peter Reid, Bob Cass and Joe Melling at a lunch – we were doing a newspaper inteview because it was just before the derby game against City. When I left I said: 'I'll be back in about two hours so if you're still here, fine. Have a good lunch.'

"When I came back in they were still sitting there.

"'Where were you?' said Cass.

"'I had a bit of a meeting,' I said.

"'How did your meeting go?'

"'Fantastic, brilliant. In fact one of the best bits of business I've done for a long, long time.'

"'You've not been buying, have you?' asked Cass. We were sitting round smoking a few cigars.

"'Yeah, I bought Eric Cantona today.'

"'Bugger off,' said Peter Reid, 'Bugger off.'

"'Honestly, I bought Eric!'

"'Oh bugger off, do me a favour, wait until Saturday.'

"Reidy knew it was a brilliant deal for us."

The signing of Eric Cantona was Fergie's masterstroke. United have won the title every year since the Frenchman arrived, except of course when he was banned. He was the catalyst; he was the difference between winning and finishing second. Indeed he was to become 'God'.

In the year or so before Cantona's arrival, however, Ferguson's dabblings in the transfer market had become increasingly pertinent. Denis Irwin had been plucked from Oldham for just £625,000, and in the summer of 1991 he bought Paul Parker for £625,000 from QPR, Andrei Kanchelskis for £650,000 from Shakhtyor Donezts, and Peter Schmeichel for £505,000 from Brondby. Looking back, paying just over

£1 million for these last two is a bit like discovering a Lowry at a car-boot sale.

"I was alerted to Andrei by a Norwegian journalist who sent me some videos of him in action. We then had him watched and I went to see him play for the Soviets against Germany. The man is a whirlwind. He had assets that merely demanded fine tuning; he has a cruiserweight's shoulders so you can't bounce him off the ball, as well as fantastic acceleration to escape defenders." Kanchelskis's decision to quit United still rankles with Ferguson. "Once he signed a new contract and realised he'd get a third of any transfer, he was off," he shrugs.

Ferguson had tried to sign Schmeichel two years earlier but he'd been under contract and the fee would have been enormous. But that had changed in 1991 and he sent Alan Hodgkinson, United's goalkeeping coach, to Denmark to watch him over six games. When he came back his report said simply: "Peter Schmeichel is the best goalkeeper in Europe." Since he signed, in 245 appearances for United, Schmeichel has kept a staggering 118 clean sheets.

Dion Dublin arrived from Cambridge United for £1 million in the summer of 1992 and moved on for £2 million two and a half years later. Then in the summer of 1993, with the hangovers from the Championship celebrations still wearing off, United broke the British transfer record to snatch Roy Keane from Nottingham Forest. It was a move which Ferguson saw "as a reminder to the rest of football that we are not going to sit back contentedly and reflect on our glory. I needed to show the players that we had to retain our hunger, be

mean as hell again. Roy, as well as being a terrific buy and long-term asset, was my banner-carrier in getting that message across. United are used to beating sporting records, so it presents no problem for me to hold another in the transfer market."

Which is why, when the team wasn't scoring goals in January 1995, Ferguson had no qualms in reaching for the cheque book again to pull off an even bigger coup than his now famous Cantona raid. In January 1995 Ferguson was chasing Collymore and Ferdinand ("the team needed freshening up, we needed an injection, a lift"). Out of the blue Kevin Keegan phoned to ask about Keith Gillespie. "I said no, but then asked about Andy Cole in passing, and he didn't dismiss it like he had earlier in the season.

"Two days later I phoned Kevin and said: 'I may be being a bit over- adventurous here, but I'm in the process of buying a striker. I just want to check that there's no way you'd sell Andy Cole to me.'

"He said: 'You've really handed me a beauty there, Alex... I wouldn't say there's no chance, but we'd really need to think about it. If you're serious, I don't know how I would respond. I sometimes feel the club isn't getting to the place I want.'

"'Well, have a think about it and come back to me,' I said.

"He rang back at four that afternoon and said: 'We'd be interested in a deal but it would need to involve Keith Gillespie.' I knew he rated Gillespie highly.

"'Well that's something I need to think about myself,' I said. So I went away to think about it with Kiddo.

"'You've got to do it,' he said. So we agreed £6 million plus Keith Gillespie, and we had Andy Cole. I couldn't believe it."

The fact that Cole's arrival didn't have quite the impact that was expected is well documented, although Ferguson is quick to defend his all-round play. "I thought Andy Cole would have scored more and I think we all expected that," he says referring to the 1995/96 campaign, "but he had one of those unfortunate seasons."

Forgetting Andy Cole's year and a half from hell, however, not one of Ferguson's major signings in the last five years has let him down. In a footballing world where money talks louder and louder, he is not concerned that the club depends to a large extent on his ability to use his cheque book well.

One transfer that in the end didn't come off was Ferguson's much-publicised courting of England's star striker Alan Shearer after Euro '96. In the end, the player ended up at arch rivals Newcastle. The deal still leaves a slightly sour taste in Ferguson's mouth.

"After speaking to him on the Monday, his agent rang me on the Thursday and I was led to believe everything was fine. The crucial part, as I understand it, was Shearer's meeting with Jack Walker. Apparently it was a very emotional meeting and Walker was practically doing somersaults whenever our name was mentioned. I think it's well documented by now that Jack Walker would never let Shearer come here because of his hatred for Manchester United. Well I've got news for Jack Walker: he's not unique. What surprises me even more is that they looked upon the fact that Shearer went to Newcastle as a victory. Try telling that to the Blackburn fans. Surely the victory would have been keeping him at Ewood Park? They used the fact he hadn't moved to Old Trafford to camouflage the sale. Maybe Blackburn fans are starting to discover now that theirs is just a small club after all."

"It used to be different when I first arrived at United, but now I bypass any impulse to carry out the soul searching and self-examination every time big money has to be spent. It can be a chilling experience when the cheque book comes out and all the noughts are penned in, but I can't concern myself strictly with the money. It's not my prime domain; the players, the overall and lasting strength of the team, have to be my priorities."

**Opposite page: Andy Cole
signs for the Reds.
Jordi Cruyff (right) and Karel Poborsky
(far right), foreign talent to
bolster Fergie's 1996/97
European Cup squad.**

Fired a

1992/93

nd inspired

The undoubted turning point of the 1992/93 season was 27 November 1992, when Alex Ferguson announced his 23rd signing for the club: a Frenchman by the name of Eric Cantona. United fans knew all about Cantona – he had arrived at Leeds earlier that year and helped them leapfrog over Man United in the closing stages of the season to win the 1991/92 Championship.

The first match after Cantona's arrival was at Highbury against Arsenal two days later. The Frenchman wasn't even playing; he was watching from the stands as his registration hadn't yet been sorted out. But the very idea of the man seemed to galvanise the United players, especially Mark Hughes, who was the obvious candidate for Cantona to replace. Hughes scored the only goal of the game.

It had been a mixed bag of a season so far. United lost their opening game at Old Trafford 3-0 to Everton and had only managed one point from their first three matches. A five-match winning run, without a single goal conceded, looked to have put them back on track. But it was followed by a run of five draws and two losses that made the previous season's Championship challenge seem light years away.

"Worrying signs first appeared at Tottenham on 19 September," says Ferguson. "We blew away incredible chances just after half time, lost concentration, and Spurs nicked the equaliser on the break." The lack of fire power up front was Ferguson's main concern, which deepened when new signing Dion Dublin broke his leg against Crystal Palace, just three games into his United career. To make matters worse, United were blasted out of the first round of the UEFA Cup by Torpedo Moscow on penalties after two 0-0 draws. Ferguson, whose voice had taken on a habitually plaintive tone, moaned: "We should have scored another sackful." Then they were dumped out of the League Cup by Aston Villa, the only goal of the game coming from Dean Saunders. Ferguson again voiced his discontent: "I don't think we have ever created more chances in a game without finding the net than in that particular tie. It was agonising to watch."

Ferguson knew he had to act or everything he'd built would crumble around him. "I wasn't going to tolerate such meagre rewards for very much longer. Once again I started sifting through the list of strikers for possible targets, with David Hirst on top of the pile." He had already looked at a certain Southampton player by the name of Alan Shearer before the end of the season, but didn't like the vibes that were coming out of Southampton, with the talks seemingly centred purely on money. "Even though in the end we didn't manage to sign him last summer," says Ferguson, "it was nice to meet Alan in person and find out the truth and good to hear his side of the story."

The pressure really started to tell when United failed to score at home to Wimbledon on 31 October. The Dons travelled back to London with a 1-0 win under their belts, courtesy of Vinnie Jones, and Ferguson's sour grapes ringing in their ears. "Wimbledon were full of it," he moaned. "They danced in the corridor to the usual ghetto blaster. The usual circus behaviour from them. It was more like a ruddy disco than a football ground."

The next week in the League at Aston Villa, Ferguson recalled Captain Marvel Bryan Robson and Lee Sharpe after injury. "Robson's big-name presence is enough and invariably he gives an extra dimension to United when he takes the field," said Ferguson. That extra dimension wasn't enough. Robson and Sharpe

**Left: Shearer at
Southampton.
Opposite page: a wet day
in Manchester, but sunshine
in Red hearts.**

weren't fully fit, United lost 1-0 and slipped to 10th place in the table. Only a series of Schmeichel saves stopped a drubbing.

United needed time to lick their wounds and, thanks to some World Cup fixtures, they got two free weeks towards the end of November. By the time they came back, Robson and Sharpe were fit again and United tore into poor Oldham. "The game against the Latics was like being transported to a different planet," says Ferguson. "We were 3-0 up at half time and the only reason we took our feet off the pedal was because Sharpe and Robson tired later in the game. But, overall, we were refreshed and the cobwebs of gloom had been blown away."

Any remaining cobwebs were swept out of sight when Cantona's signing was announced and a rejuvenated United took three points from their match at Arsenal. Then came the best stage possible for Cantona to make his debut: the Manchester derby. Eric started the game on the bench, but was brought on at half time for Ryan Giggs. "He transformed the game and the crowd loved him," recalls Ferguson. United won 2-1. Ferguson's team were on something of a roll by now, and it was just as well, because next up were Norwich City at Old Trafford. Mike Walker's team were flying high, top of the Premiership and nine points clear of United. Hughes cut that to six with a well-taken goal. Ferguson was relieved. "Somebody had to peg them back before they escaped and ran clear. It was vital we stopped their gallop, and we did."

By 9 January, United were top of the table. They'd showed a great deal of flair by beating Coventry 5-0 and Spurs 4-1 on either side of the New Year. The real pointer to their new-found determination, however, came in the 3-3 draw they shared with Sheffield Wednesday at Hillsborough on Boxing Day. United came back after being 3-0 down. "Over the last few years I have shared in few Manchester United matches of that level of high drama and calibre," said Ferguson afterwards. "It's always a fabulous feeling to have been involved in the sort of football entertainment on which United's image and reputation has been created."

United marched on despite the odd hiccup – including defeats by Ipswich at Portman Road and Sheffield United in the FA Cup fifth round at Bramall Lane. Ferguson believed the latter result to be a blessing in disguise, even though he thought United might have had two more penalties than the one Bruce missed. "That was arguably the greatest favour the ref could grant us," said Ferguson. "Last season we did Leeds a big

**The pain (opposite page):
Bruce misses at Bramall Lane.
The glory (right):
Bruce's two late goals beat
Sheffield Wednesday.**

favour when we knocked them out of both Cups. This year there won't be any fixture pile-up for us." Another advantage he detected over the year before was a new attitude among his players. "I felt they were stronger and better equipped for the task ahead in 1993. We had been down that road once and weren't scared of the route any more. Experience is one of the footballer's greatest allies."

United certainly needed to dig deep to beat Sheffield Wednesday on 10 April. When Aston Villa, who had emerged as United's only serious Championship rivals, finished their match with Coventry, United were losing 1-0. By the time they were out of the team bath, Ferguson's men had turned the game round 2-1. Bruce was the hero, scoring the equaliser with four minutes on the clock and the winner in the seventh minute of injury time that the referee had allowed. "It should have been 12, mind you," said Ferguson afterwards.

United were on a winning streak and scaring the daylights out of Villa. They beat Coventry 1-0, Chelsea 3-0 and Crystal Palace 2-0 to go four points clear with two games left.

When Aston Villa played Oldham live on TV on Sunday 2 May, they knew that a win or a draw would keep them in with a sniff and a defeat would hand the title to United. So did Ferguson, although he had decided he could do without the pressure and was having a quiet round of golf with his son Mark instead of watching the match. He was on the 17th hole, assuming that Villa had won, when he was approached by a complete stranger. "'Mr. Ferguson?' he asked," recounts Ferguson. "'They murdered Villa, Oldham have won. It's all over. United are Champions.'" Fergie never made it to the 18th hole.

For Ferguson, it was more than just a trophy. It was the first time in 26 years that Manchester United had won the League, and he'd been the man to guide them to it. "The afternoon of 2 May 1993, when we were crowned the champions of England, was the day I truly became manager of Manchester United," he says. "It was the historic moment when I could finally realise, even inwardly accept, that I was the man in charge."

1992/93

Back row: Andrei Kanchelskis, Mike Phelan, Eric Cantona, Peter Schmeichel, Les Sealey, Gary Pallister, Dion Dublin, Lee Sharpe.   **Middle row:** Norman Davies, Brian McClair, Denis Irwin, Ryan Giggs, Lee Martin, Darren Ferguson, Roy Keane, Mark Hughes, Jim McGregor.
Front row: Danny Wallace, Clayton Blackmore, Alex Ferguson, Steve Bruce, Bryan Robson, Brian Kidd, Paul Ince, Paul Parker.

Premiership											
Aug 15	(a)	Sheffield U	L	1-2	Hughes	Jan 27	(h)	Notts Forest	W	2-0	Ince, Hughes
Aug 19	(h)	Everton	L	0-3		Jan 30	(a)	Ipswich T	L	1-2	McClair
Aug 22	(h)	Ipswich T	D	1-1	Irwin	Feb 6	(h)	Sheffield U	W	2-1	McClair, Cantona
Aug 24	(a)	South'ton	W	1-0	Dublin	Feb 8	(a)	Leeds U	D	0-0	
Aug 29	(a)	Notts Forest	W	2-0	Hughes, Giggs	Feb 20	(h)	South'ton	W	2-1	Giggs 2
Sep 2	(h)	Crystal P	W	1-0	Hughes	Feb 27	(h)	Middlesbro	W	3-0	Giggs, Irwin, Cantona
Sep 6	(h)	Leeds U	W	2-0	Kanchelskis, Bruce	Mar 6	(a)	Liverpool	W	2-1	Hughes, McClair
						Mar 9	(a)	Oldham A	L	0-1	
Sep 12	(a)	Everton	W	2-0	McClair, Bruce	Mar 14	(h)	Aston Villa	D	1-1	Hughes
Sep 19	(a)	Tottenham	D	1-1	Giggs	Mar 20	(a)	Man City	D	1-1	Cantona
Sep 26	(h)	QPR	D	0-0		Mar 24	(h)	Arsenal	D	0-0	
Oct 3	(a)	Middlesbro	D	1-1	Bruce	Apr 5	(a)	Norwich C	W	3-1	Giggs, Cantona, Kanchelskis,
Oct 18	(h)	Liverpool	D	2-2	Hughes 2						
Oct 24	(a)	Blackburn	D	0-0		Apr 10	(h)	Sheff Wed	W	2-1	Bruce 2
Oct 31	(h)	Wimbledon	L	0-1		Apr 12	(a)	Coventry C	W	1-0	Irwin
Nov 7	(a)	Aston Villa	L	0-1		Apr 17	(h)	Chelsea	W	3-0	Hughes, Clarke, Cantona
Nov 21	(h)	Oldham A	W	3-0	McClair 2, Hughes	Apr 21	(a)	Crystal P	W	2-0	Hughes, Ince
Nov 28	(a)	Arsenal	W	1-0	Hughes	May 3	(h)	Blackburn	W	3-1	Giggs, Ince, Pallister
Dec 6	(h)	Man City	W	2-1	Ince, Hughes						
Dec 12	(h)	Norwich C	W	1-0	Hughes	May 9	(a)	Wimbledon	W	2-1	Ince, Robson
Dec 10	(a)	Chelsea	D	1-1	Cantona	**Final League position: first in Premier League**					
Dec 26	(a)	Sheff Wed	D	3-3	McClair 2, Cantona						
Dec 28	(h)	Coventry C	W	5-0	Giggs, Hughes, Cantona, Sharpe, Irwin	**FA Cup**					
						3rd round					
						Jan 5	(h)	Bury	W	2-0	Phelan, Gillespie
Jan 9	(h)	Tottenham	W	4-1	Cantona, Irwin, McClair, Parker	4th Round					
						Jan 23	(h)	Brighton	W	1-0	Giggs
Jan 18	(a)	QPR	W	3-1	Ince, Giggs, Kanchelskis	5th Round					
						Feb 14	(a)	Sheffield U	L	1-2	Giggs

The

King and I

In August 1995 Alex Ferguson flew to Paris and booked into the George V Hotel. He wasn't alone. There were pressmen everywhere, the same men who had been plastering the back pages of their papers with "Eric for Inter" stories for weeks. Ferguson's mission was to try and hang on to a player whose momentary aberration against a Crystal Palace fan at

When Alex Ferguson talks about Eric Cantona he speaks like he's describing some great painting or a magnificent statue. Over the last five years the two have built up an immensely strong bond based on mutual admiration and respect. Ferguson has found the player of his dreams and Cantona has at last found somewhere in the footballing world which he can call home.

"He is the most talented, the most influential player I've ever signed in terms of impact on the football team, the support and the game as a whole," says Ferguson. "He has such presence about him – an aura – as well as a fantastic work ethic. He contributes so much to a game. He scores goals, creates goals and dreams up little miracles that are simply beyond the technical scope and imagination of most people. His vision and touch around the box sometimes stretch my belief."

Fergie flew all the way to Paris for dinner on that August evening as a measure of how much he valued the Frenchman. "Not long after I arrived, Eric's lawyer Jean-Jacques Bertrand turned up on a motorbike," he recalls. "We sneaked out of the back door, I jumped on the back of the bike and we drove across Paris. I had one of those helmets on. It was quite exciting really.

"We met at a restaurant owned by a friend of Eric's, who closed it for us, and the four of us had a lovely meal. Eric and I talked about great games of the past. His knowledge of football is amazing – World Cups of the Fifties and Sixties as well as European Cup Finals.

"At the start of pre-season a few weeks earlier, I had called him in and told him exactly what I had planned to do with him. I told him I had arranged a number of behind-closed-door friendlies which would give him two games a week until his suspension ended in October. He was delighted. Then the FA acted on the evidence of a cameraman at the first session after he got a tip-off from someone at one of the housing developments which surround the training ground. His pictures were in the papers and that led to some smartass at the FA saying: 'Cantona can't do this, he's banned from all football.' It was ridiculous.

"It all got to him. His wife had just had a baby and he was living in a hotel. I went to see him and he was disgusted at being banned from these closed matches. He was sitting in his room on his own, taking his meals on his own. And I said: 'This is crazy, you should be in your house.' That was one thing, and then he was saying perhaps he should go back to France and I was half agreeing with him, because I was disgusted with the FA decision myself.

"He said he'd had enough, and I can understand that – people can only take so much. He'd done his community service, he'd taken his FA ban, he'd never said a word, but he took it. He decided to go back to France, but I spoke to his lawyer and we both agreed that we weren't going to accept this situation and that we could talk our way around this.

"So when I met Eric in the restaurant that night I was able to tell him that I'd had some joy out of the FA. I told him that they'd said he could play the games as long as we didn't make them 'official' friendlies.

We could play 40-minute matches, or three halves of half an hour, and that would be OK. As soon as I told him that there was no problem anymore, there was no more discussion, and no question that he'd return to play for us. I think he'd settled down by then, he'd been with his wife, and the news I gave him was important. To be honest I don't think Inter Milan ever came into it... and it gave us all a boost to know he was staying."

Ferguson had invested so much in Cantona. He'd staked the reputation of the whole club on him by standing by him after his Selhurst Park abomination. Now Cantona was paying him back.

"We signed Eric so quickly in 1992," continues Ferguson. "But after the press conference I started to get jitters about the whole business. Not quite panic, but an uncertainty as to whether we had done the right thing. I began worrying about all the controversial stuff being traded around about Eric's past. A couple of Leeds players were quoted and a few innuendoes started to filter from Elland Road about him. It looked like a fair amount of propaganda to me. It seemed to be a smokescreen to placate Leeds fans who were wondering why one of their favourite players had been sold to a deadly rival.

"The situation upset me, but not for more than a few hours. It was always my committed belief that this was the club to suit Cantona perfectly. Some players, many with respected and established reputations, are cowed and broken by the size and expectations of the place. Not Eric. He swaggered in, stuck his chest out, raised his head and surveyed everything as though he was asking: 'I'm Cantona, how big are you? Are you big enough for me?' The question, I've got to say, is usually posed the other way round. I knew at that precise moment I could banish all my fears about him.

"He is the true theatrical performer. The more important the performance, the more he is inspired by it. He's also the best prepared footballer I've ever had. He's first out on the training pitch, he does his own warm-up and then he does our warm-up. He trains brilliantly, and then he practices after training and he's the last to leave the car park, signing autographs. He's a model pro, an absolute dream footballer."

But Fergie's dream nearly turned into a nightmare on that blustery night at Selhurst Park on 25 January 1995. "I saw him walking towards the tunnel and turned my attention back to the field after he'd been sent off. Then I heard this commotion and turned to see Eric spread-eagled across the hoarding. I thought that a fan had pulled him across the boards and into the crowd as he walked past.

"We didn't have a clear picture about what had happened but after the game we were called into the referee's room to talk to the police and we were told there would be an investigation."

When Fergie got home late that night, his son Jason told him: "You'll not believe it. He karate kicked the guy," but Ferguson went straight to bed. "I just lay there wondering what he had done," he remembers. "At 5.25 am I got up and put the video on. I couldn't believe what I saw."

Ferguson describes how "the air was filled with an overriding sense of doom" the next day at Old Trafford. He met with the chairman Martin Edwards, the chairman of the Manchester United plc Sir Roland Smith and the club's lawyer Maurice Watkins. "I felt that it would be almost impossible for Eric to stay with the club, because of the media coverage we have and because of provocation by opponents. But as the meeting went on and we discussed it, we realised it was more important to satisfy ourselves than the rest of the world. What was right for Manchester United was the most important factor. The action we took indicated we didn't accept what he did, but – more importantly – the club did what was right for the supporters."

And when Cantona made his triumphant return in October 1996 – with Old Trafford awash with tricolour flags and Eric on his best behaviour – that January night seemed a long way off. And the Frenchman's subsequent exemplary behaviour both on and off the pitch has vindicated his manager's decision to stand by him.

Now Ferguson talks of the "rejuvenated Cantona" in more glowing terms than ever. Sir Bobby Charlton realised the power of his words after the FA Cup Final when he said: "He's as good a player as we've ever had here." As the stack of trophies piles up around him, Ferguson puts it quite simply. "Cantona makes the difference," he says.

Double

1993/94

champions

A remarkable thing happened on 11 September 1993. Manchester United lost. To Chelsea. Non-United football fans all over the country breathed a sigh of relief: Ferguson's men were men, and not machines. Until that point they'd looked simply unstoppable, winning five out of their first six matches and drawing the other (with Newcastle). Eric Cantona saw Glenn Hoddle as the difference between the teams. "In the modern game there are few great musicians," he said after the game. "But Hoddle is like Mozart among the hard rock men." Ferguson, of course, was more prosaic, blaming defeat on the fact that most of his players were tired after World Cup duty. "The effects of the midweek international matches definitely began to show in the first 20 minutes when we seemed to be second to every ball," he said. "That's the price of having so many international players in the squad." Chelsea were to figure quite heavily in United's season that year.

In the six years he had been at the club, Ferguson had brought in an entirely new team. Only Bryan Robson remained from those dark early days in the Eighties. Every member of the team who went to Stamford Bridge, apart from Steve Bruce, was a full international. The team against Chelsea – Schmeichel, Parker, Irwin, Bruce, Pallister, Sharpe, Ince, Keane, Robson, Giggs, Cantona – had an air of invincibility about it that put fear in the hearts of opposition. Against Chelsea, McClair and Kanchelskis were on the bench. Hughes was in the stands. It no longer looked like a question of whether United were up to winning the Championship any more. It had become a question of who the hell could stop them?

United marched on after their Stamford Bridge hiccup. At the end of September they were three points clear of Arsenal at the top of the table. At the end of October they were 11 points clear of Norwich City, having won 11 of their 13 games. The only blot on their copy-book was an over-confident performance against Galatasaray in the European Cup second round. United took a 2-0 Old Trafford lead after 13 minutes and looked to have settled the tie, but Galatasaray fought back and stunned Old Trafford with three goals. United's long, proud unbeaten-in-Europe home record was under threat until Cantona forced the ball into the net on 81 minutes. Ferguson was furious after the match. "Our carelessness is destroying our potential," he said afterwards. "As soon as we went 2-0 up, two or three of our players started to run with the ball, treating the match like a one man show, and we just stopped playing as a team."

The next leg took place two weeks later. A trip to Galatasaray might be put in the 'difficult away matches' category. "Welcome to Hell" was the message from the Turkish fans. United simply didn't gel on the night and, on a night they needed a win or an extraordinarily high score draw, failed even to get one goal. "We did not play well, and when desperation crept in, the whole thing became a shambles," said Ferguson after the game.

Their League campaign was anything but a shambles. After Galatasaray there was a Maine Road derby to put the mind right back on matters English. City had the temerity to go 2-0 up at half time. But it wasn't enough. "The score at half time was a travesty and I simply told our lads in the interval to keep playing their football and it would come right. Eric's performance showed the sheer intelligence of the man. He knew exactly what was needed to cope with City's sweeper system and he came up with two goals as well," commented Fergie. Roy Keane added a third with three minutes to go, and three more points were in the bag.

By the end of November, United were 14 points clear of Leeds. By Christmas, Blackburn Rovers had established themselves as United's main rivals. United still looked unbeatable, but had started dropping points by drawing games: at Old Trafford against Ipswich and Norwich, for example, and at St James Park. So it was vital for their morale that they defeated Rovers at Old Trafford in the Boxing Day six pointer. Kevin Gallacher scored early for Blackburn, and the visitors then closed the game down. United tried desperately for the equaliser, but in vain – until the 88th minute. Paul Ince toe-poked a Sharpe corner into the net after Schmeichel had disrupted the Rovers defence with a crazy run from his own goal. "I didn't think we'd get the point," said Ferguson, "but we managed to claw back through sheer desperation, and the desire to preserve our home record." Not the victory they needed to pull 16 points clear, but a moral victory nonetheless after snatching a draw from the jaws of defeat.

The New Year signalled the start of the FA Cup, and United kicked off their 1994 campaign with a tricky away tie at Bramall Lane. "The heaviness of the pitch might have meant that a shock was on the cards," says Ferguson. "We found it hard to string our passes together in the first half, but I felt we matched their

Top: Cantona inspires
United's comeback in the
Maine Road derby.
Above: Ince's last-ditch
equaliser against Blackburn.

Top: the turning point.
Sparky equalises in the
FA Cup semi final.
Left: the Final, and Hughes shields the ball.
Above: Saunders' penalty sinks
United's treble hopes.

determination." In the second half, United came out of their shells and Mark Hughes scored a 62 minute killer-goal that was enough to put United into the fourth round. A win at Portsmouth in the fifth round of the Coca-Cola Cup – after a 2-2 draw at Old Trafford – meant that United were now attacking on three fronts, and the treble looked a distinct possibility. A superbly professional performance in the FA Cup fourth round saw United leave Carrow Road with a 2-0 win. "Who can stop this red machine?" asked the *Sun*, and nobody had an answer. A 5-1 aggregate win over Sheffield Wednesday in the Coca-Cola Cup semi final and a 3-0 annihilation of Wimbledon in the fifth round of the FA Cup, followed by a sixth round win over Charlton, saw United looking very much a Cup-winning team.

United's league campaign was going well throughout the Cup run, but points were still being dropped, and Blackburn were, if not snapping at their heels, at least chomping at their coat tails. At the end of March, when United lost 1-0 at home to their bogey team Chelsea, their 34-match unbeaten run ended and their lead was cut to six points.

By that time, the treble dreams were over. For the second time in three years Ron Atkinson thwarted Ferguson's League Cup campaign. This time it was Aston Villa he was managing, and they out-thought United to win 3-1. "I have no argument with the result," says Ferguson. "Villa set out with very clever tactics, took the lead and defended it brilliantly." To make matters worse, United travelled to Blackburn six days later and were beaten – by two Alan Shearer goals to nil. The gap was down to three points. "This result makes it a lot more interesting now," said Ferguson. "We know exactly what we have to do."

What they didn't want to do was go and lose at Wimbledon, which would let Blackburn catch up with them on 79 points. "We made a bad mistake to concede the goal, but at the same time we were at fault at the other end of the pitch for not creating anything. The League title race will go right to the wire now," said Ferguson. He then told United to put their foot full down on the throttle. In the next two weeks United beat Manchester City, Leeds, Ipswich and Southampton to put the pressure firmly on Rovers. On 2 May, Rovers lost to Coventry, and United had won their second title on the trot.

The treble had been forgotten, and the double looked a goner with United 1-0 down to Oldham late into the FA Cup semi final. But Hughes unleashed a huge volley in the 88th minute, and a 4-1 replay win set United up for the Final against Chelsea, who had already beaten United 2-0. You'll remember what happened. Chelsea played well but were beaten 4-0, and the double was Manchester United's, for the first time.

The frightening thing was that after winning the Championship in 1993, United made winning the double look almost easy. "With 26 years of frustration over we could approach our task with a clear mind," says Ferguson. "The fans were much more relaxed and the big challenge for the players was to put real authority into their game, to dominate English football. Without question they achieved that."

**The first man to score
two penalties in an FA Cup Final.**

Ferguson's tribute to Sir Matt Busby

On 20 January 1994, the football world in general and Manchester United in particular was shocked to hear of the death of Sir Matt Busby. He was the greatest manager ever at Old Trafford and had brought home the European Cup in the era of Charlton, Law and Best. Ferguson paid tribute to his most illustrious predecessor. "He was an incredible man and a fantastic manager. In my estimation he was the outstanding man of them all – even Bill Shankly and Jock Stein sought his experience and advice. He stood above everybody and he will be sorely missed at Old Trafford. Sir Matt was a tremendous influence on me, as he was on everyone at Old Trafford. His mere presence about the place was enough to motivate people, to generate a pride in what you were doing. When he used to come on to the team coach with us for away matches, you could see the players nudging each other and saying 'Look, there's Sir Matt.' Even as he grew older he would come into the club every day, and though maybe he didn't recognise everyone any more he always had time for you. He had a knack of saying 'Hello, son' or 'Hello, dear,' in a way which made you feel important."

Two days after his death United faced Everton at home and beat them, 1-0, at a highly emotional Old Trafford. "I think Sir Matt would have been proud of the way we played today – we played some wonderful football, and showed great speed and movement. It was very hard for both teams in the first half after the minute's silence, which was incredibly moving for everybody at Old Trafford. I told the players before the game that what was important was to enjoy the game and put on a good show in the style that would have pleased Sir Matt. I think they achieved that today."

1993/94

Back row: Andrei Kanchelskis, Roy Keane, Lee Sharpe, Denis Irwin, Ryan Giggs, Paul Ince, Bryan Robson, Gary Pallister, Les Sealey, Eric Cantona.
Front row: Darren Ferguson, Peter Schmeichel, Steve Bruce, Paul Parker, Mark Hughes, Brian McClair, Brian Kidd.

Premiership

Aug 15	(a)	Norwich C	W	2-0	Robson, Giggs
Aug 18	(h)	Sheffield U	W	3-0	Keane 2, Hughes
Aug 21	(h)	Newcastle U	D	1-1	Giggs
Aug 23	(a)	Aston Villa	W	2-1	Sharpe 2
Aug 28	(a)	South'ton	W	3-1	Irwin, Sharpe, Cantona
Sep 1	(h)	West Ham	W	3-0	Bruce, Sharpe, Cantona
Sep 11	(a)	Chelsea	L	0-1	
Sep 19	(h)	Arsenal	W	1-0	Cantona
Sep 25	(h)	Swindon T	W	4-2	Cantona, Hughes 2, Kanchelskis
Oct 2	(a)	Sheff Wed	W	3-2	Hughes 2, Giggs
Oct 16	(h)	Tottenham	W	2-1	Sharpe, Keane
Oct 23	(a)	Everton	W	1-0	Sharpe
Oct 30	(h)	QPR	W	2-1	Cantona, Hughes
Nov 7	(a)	Man City	W	3-2	Cantona 2, Keane
Nov 20	(h)	Wimbledon	W	3-1	Pallister, Hughes Kanchelskis
Nov 24	(h)	Ipswich T	D	0-0	
Nov 27	(a)	Coventry C	W	1-0	Cantona
Dec 4	(h)	Norwich C	D	2-2	McClair, Giggs
Dec 7	(a)	Sheffied U	W	3-0	Sharpe, Cantona, Hughes
Dec 11	(a)	Newcastle U	D	1-1	Ince
Dec 19	(h)	Aston Villa	W	3-1	Cantona 2, Ince
Dec 26	(h)	Blackburn	D	1-1	Ince
Dec 29	(a)	Oldham A	W	5-2	Bruce, Kanchelskis Giggs 2, Cantona
Jan 1	(h)	Leeds U	D	0-0	
Jan 4	(a)	Liverpool	D	3-3	Irwin, Bruce, Giggs
Jan 15	(a)	Tottenham	W	1-0	Hughes
Jan 22	(h)	Everton	W	1-0	Giggs
Feb 5	(a)	QPR	W	3-2	Kanchelskis, Cantona, Giggs
Feb 26	(a)	West Ham	D	2-2	Ince, Hughes
Mar 5	(h)	Chelsea	L	0-1	
Mar 14	(h)	Sheff Wed	W	5-0	Cantona 2, Ince Hughes, Giggs
Mar 19	(a)	Swindon T	D	2-2	Keane, Ince
Mar 22	(a)	Arsenal	D	2-2	Sharpe 2
Mar 30	(h)	Liverpool	W	1-0	Ince
Apr 2	(a)	Blackburn	L	0-2	
Apr 4	(h)	Oldham A	W	3-2	Ince, Giggs, Dublin
Apr 16	(a)	Wimbledon	L	0-1	
Apr 23	(h)	Man City	W	2-0	Cantona 2
Apr 27	(a)	Leeds U	W	2-0	Kanchelskis, Giggs
May 1	(a)	Ipswich T	W	2-1	Cantona, Giggs
May 4	(h)	South'ton	W	2-0	Kanchelskis, Hughes
May 8	(h)	Coventry C	D	0-0	

Final League position: first in FA Premiership

FA Cup

3rd Round

Jan 9	(a)	Sheffield U	W	1-0	Hughes

4th Round

Jan 30	(a)	Norwich C	W	2-0	Keane, Cantona

5th Round

Feb 20th	(a)	Wimbledon	W	3-0	Irwin, Cantona, Ince

6th Round

Mar 12	(h)	Charlton A	W	3-1	Kanchelskis 2, Hughes

Semi-Final

Apr 10	Oldham A	D	1-1	Hughes

Replay

Apr 13	Oldham A	W	4-1	Irwin, Kanchelskis, Robson, Giggs

Final

May 14	Chelsea	W	4-0	Cantona 2, Hughes, McClair

European Champions' Cup

1st Round (1st Leg)

Sep 15	(a)	Honved	W	3-2	Cantona, Keane 2

1st Round (2nd Leg)

Sep 29	(h)	Honved	W	2-1	Bruce 2

2nd Round (1st Leg)

Oct 20	(h)	Galatasaray	D	3-3	Robson, Hakan, Cantona

2nd Round (2nd Leg)

Nov 3	(a)	Galatasaray	D	0-0	

Fergie's

strengths

With a roll of honour longer than the queue for season tickets at Old Trafford, Alex Ferguson's managerial record speaks for itself. Uncomfortable with self-congratulation and prolonged reflection on a successful career, he prefers instead to look to the future and make sure that he continues to build on his past glory.

"I'm not interested in crowing," says Alex Ferguson. "Winning the double again in 1996 was great for the players and the supporters but we've got to carry on winning. As soon as one season is over, the most important thing is the next one.

"I spent six-and-a-half years securing the Championship, and the club was locked into 26 years of title failure before it was accomplished, so nobody kids us about the glory game. All that gritty experience and heartache teaches you not to make off-the-cuff predictions about sweeping the board, being the best in the land and all that stuff. All it does, anyway, is increase the hostility of rival teams and their supporters.

"When the players believe they have cracked it, that the game is easy, it's my job to bring them crashing back to reality. All I have to say is that it's tea-cup time. I don't even need to grab hold of the old dressing-room china these days. Just mention the word and the players are ducking for cover. I'm sorry to spoil the popular myth but, in truth, I haven't slung a tea cup for years. The last pot shot was at Gordon Strachan and I missed him, so I wish the wee man would stop moaning about it.

"I do explode like a volcano at times and that gets rid of all the strain and tension of my workload and pressures. Jock Stein, of course, was quite the opposite. I still remember Jock, in that slow, lazy drawl of his, advising me: 'Hey son, leave the big stuff till Monday; it will be nice and calm by then.' But I never could wait another minute, never mind until Monday. It's a violent emotion and I must release it fast. I believe it's good for you to rid the system of all that deep-down anger. Put all the cards on the table, tell the players exactly how you feel, and the next day it's a different, wonderful world."

Ferguson claims he is lucky that he can switch off from football at will ("I couldn't have survived this long without being able to do that"), but perhaps the main secret of his success is that he doesn't seem to want to. "My all consuming passion is football," he says. "Always has been, always will be. I'm not a golfer or a hill-walker, and I don't go down the pub for a pint or a pipe to relax. I owned a pub, it's true, but I haven't been in one since I was a very young man. My whole objective is to work hard to make certain I have a job for life at United."

Ultimately, Ferguson has thrived at United because of the size of the club and the size of the task. A man seemingly born to climb metaphorical mountains all his life – always insisting the bigger the better – he revels in the unique problems thrown up by managing the biggest club in the land.

"We now exist in a highly charged, black-and-white, cut-throat game. There are times when you have to be brutal – there's no better word for it. Moments when decisions must be delivered that crush people. It is always down to you to tell players when their career is over, for example, when they have to be left out or it is simply time for them to move on. People are full of advice, but they don't have to tell Mark Hughes or Bryan Robson that they're not going to play. Neither my assistants, nor the chairman, nor any supporter ever had to go to Bryan and say: 'Oh Bryan, you're not playing in the Cup Final.' That's my job and you sometimes get pilloried for it."

OK, here it comes, the oldest cliché in football... no one man is bigger than Manchester United. Ferguson took his risk with Cantona all right, but at the root of his reasoning, as always, was the good of the team. Despite his portrayal as a maverick genius, Cantona is in fact the epitome of a team player – carrying out his manager's instructions to the last, training obsessively and preparing himself immaculately for every game. In the summer of 1995, Paul Ince was allowed to leave for Inter Milan. A shock departure at the time, but Ferguson insists now that Ince was starting to display less of a dedication to the cause and more of a dedication to Paul Ince.

"I felt it was important we had control of the dressing room and also the tension within the team," he says, explaining why he allowed the £6-million deal to go through. "I mean I can pick the 11 best players I've had at this club and may not win a game of football; to win games of football you need a team understanding and a cause that gets everyone to relate to each other. The minute that breaks down you're trying to fit parts or plug gaps and it all starts to fall apart. I think we lost in Barcelona, Gothenburg and at Anfield that 1994/95 season through lack of attention to the team cause. Ince was going forward more and more, he

wasn't listening to my instructions, and I had Nicky Butt, Roy Keane and David Beckham in reserve.

"In fact I think that the change has been good for Paul, and since moving to Inter Milan I think he has grown in stature. I was delighted to see his performances for England in Euro '96, doing what he does best – sitting in front of the back four, tackling, organising and using the ball superbly once he's won it."

The team is always all-important and Ferguson likes to create a close-knit squad, encourage team outings and foster a lively dressing-room atmosphere. "I love going in and hearing the banter when they arrive for training," he explains. "They all wonder what I'm doing there. They think I'm checking up on how they dress in the morning, or if I can smell drink, but I just love the banter."

And when he's got his own team sorted, he'll start thinking about the opposition – and if that means winding the other side up, then so be it. The image of Kevin Keegan hurling his Sky headphones to the ground in an outburst directed at Ferguson after Newcastle played Leeds is one of the enduring memories of the last campaign.

"I wanted to focus on Leeds because I felt most people in the game thought they were letting their manager down," explains Ferguson. "Howard is a friend of mine. There was a lot of speculation about his future at Leeds and he was getting some reaction from the fans. I think most people in the game felt his players were letting him down. There is such bitter rivalry between us and Leeds that I was just a bit concerned they'd be walking into that game quite happy maybe for New... " Fergie stops himself. "I don't know, you have that feeling in the back of your mind that there's no foot on the gas, they're quite happy if Newcastle win the league. So I focused attention on the fact that they could produce this great performance against us and run three times the distance they might normally run all season. And was I supposed to let them off with that? Maybe it made them sit up and think they should be doing better for their manager. And that the team should be far higher up the league than they were and not down in a relegation battle.

"The way they played against us annoyed me. It seems they hate us so much they can produce that performance and yet in the last 20 games since they've played us they've been idling as far as a lot of people are concerned, particularly the Leeds fans. So I made the point after the game. First of all I said that Howard didn't deserve this treatment and then I said I hoped they would produce something against Newcastle.

"I was watching on TV after the game when Newcastle played Leeds and I just think Kevin was under tremendous pressure. I felt the pressure on ourselves at times, but you have to try and control yourself. I just think the emotions got to Kevin because he's an emotional guy – he wears his heart on his sleeve. We get on fine now, there are no problems. In fact we haven't talked about it.

"The year before I was trying to bring psychology into the Blackburn chase, saying they'd cracked and that we were going to catch them. That was different because I knew Blackburn had great resilience, they were determined buggers and were going to clubs just determined to get something out of the game. They weren't interested in entertaining, and that was a difference between them and Newcastle."

Ferguson has made winning, and entertaining, his business, but to continue to satisfy both criteria he knows he can never rest on his laurels. "As a manager you can't afford too many off days. But self-examination is vital if you are going to succeed. I have to constantly assess myself and my preparation. Did I pick the right team? Were the tactics right? The other vital thing is to respond to adversity rather than lapsing into depression. I remember a manager who had never touched a drop of alcohol in his life until he became manager of St Mirren. He ended up drinking a bottle a day."

So close...

On the 22 January 1995, Manchester United beat Blackburn Rovers 1–0 in a vital six-pointer. It was billed as the Championship decider between the two clubs who were the only obvious contenders for the Premiership title. The goalscorer for United, of course, was Eric Cantona. "He seems to have settled down and now knows where his destiny lies. His last six performances have been magnificent for us," said Ferguson after the match. Three days later United travelled to Crystal Palace. You all know what happened next.

BARCELONA 4
MANCHESTER 0
STOITCHKOV (2)
10 ROMARIO
FERRER

Barça away: United's 1994/95 invasion of Europe is repelled.

One person who didn't get a clear view of the incident was Alex Ferguson, who went to bed that night unsure of what the fuss was all about. When he eventually saw a video recording of the event early the next morning, he was shocked to witness Eric Cantona, after he was sent off, losing his rag and launching himself feet first at an abusive spectator in the crowd.

"On Sunday Eric took us to heaven with that wonderful goal to beat Blackburn. Three days later we have been taken to hell," said Ferguson, before suspending Cantona until the end of the season. The FA's reaction was even harsher: Cantona was banned from football for eight months. It was to prove the crucial moment in United's season.

The previous season United attacked on three fronts after being knocked out of the UEFA Cup early. This time round they were attacking on four, as they automatically qualified for a place in the European Champions' League. It cast doubts in Ferguson's mind, as he still remembered the havoc that fixture congestion played with his first title challenge in 1992. The League Cup was obviously bottom on his list of priorities, but he came up with a compromise. He started fielding young, inexperienced players in the competition, the likes of Butt, Beckham, Scholes, Neville, Gillespie and Davies. "I have no doubts about their ability or their temperament," he said. The kids beat Port Vale over two legs, but Newcastle away was a different proposition. "I've never been into a game in my life wanting to lose. But I've got two chambers in my mind working. One is telling me, 'Alex, don't go for the League Cup, forget about it,' and the other is saying 'getting beaten is not on the agenda of Manchester United.'" United lost the Newcastle game to two late goals, but Ferguson was pleased with his new brood of fledglings. "It was a pleasure to see they had the confidence to play one-twos just outside the penalty box to get themselves out of trouble."

The European Champions' League, however, was a kettle of rather more dangerous fish. United started well, with a 4-2 win over Gothenburg which put two vital points in the bank but showed how vulnerable the defence was. "My main feeling about the match is one of relief," said Ferguson afterwards. "Starting with a win was vital. Nine points will get us through for certain, eight points should do it. That win gives us a cushion." Galatasaray away was the next fixture – one that United players were familiar with after the season before. Again the match finished 0-0 and United's challenge was still on course. Next up were Barcelona at Old Trafford. The day before the match, United had a rehearsal with the Reserves playing the part of Barcelona. "Paul Scholes took the role of Romario, but he twice spotted Peter Schmeichel off his line and chipped him. Peter went mad," says Fergie. The real Catalans were a different proposition, though, and were 2-1 up with 12 minutes to go. Then United upped the tempo, and Sharpe equalised with a magnificent back-heel flick. Honours were even. "Today's match was one of the most exciting I've ever been involved in," said Ferguson afterwards. "The great thing about European football is that it seems to extend your life. I always seem to go to bed later after European matches because of the adrenalin buzz they give me."

United had wanted a win, but a draw would do if they could get some sort of a result in the return match in Spain on 9 November. Ferguson, hamstrung by the three foreigner rule, dropped Schmeichel and put Gary Walsh in his place. United were humiliated 4-0. "All I can say is that it was a bad, bad performance," was Ferguson's reaction afterwards. "I'm sure my players were thinking," he continued, "but it makes me wonder whether they were really listening. Perhaps they need these bitter lessons all the time. Keeping the ball is the name of the game in Europe and they just don't understand. We don't have a tactical game in England. The problem at United is that a lot of players have their own profile and want to play their own way. It doesn't work in Europe, as we've discovered." They proved it by losing 3-1 at Gothenburg to effectively go out of the competition, despite rallying in the last match to beat Galatasaray 4-0.

Still, there was the little matter of the double to consider. United's league campaign had been going pretty well. The highlights before Christmas were the biggest win over Manchester City for more than 100 years, and victories over major rivals Newcastle and Blackburn, 2-0 and 4-2 at Old Trafford and Ewood Park respectively. The low points were a home defeat by Nottingham Forest on 16 November and a defeat at Elland Road in September. "The Leeds supporters were awful," recalls Ferguson. "Such hatred really is incredible. Apparently, a TV camera caught some woman screaming abuse at me. When it gets to women behaving in that way what chance have you got?"

After the Cantona incident in January, United really had their work cut out. They set about chasing Blackburn with some determination. February saw straight wins over Villa, Manchester City, Leeds and Norwich before a 1-0 defeat at Everton. Then came the showpiece match. Ipswich had been leaking goals all season but they didn't know what hit them on 4 March. United scored nine, five of them from new-ish boy Andy Cole. "I didn't want them to score 10," says Ferguson, "because it's unthinkable for a manager to lose

**Cloud nine: five for
Andy Cole against Ipswich.**

10-0. At the end of the game George [Burley] was really emotional. I went across and said 'Look I'm sorry about that, but you just have to do it.' He just walked away. He never came in for a drink, and I can understand that. But it was a marvellous performance – you could have set it to music."

The title race went right to the wire and ended up with a nail-biting finish. United, to make the Championship theirs, had to win against West Ham, and hope that Blackburn didn't win at Liverpool.

Meanwhile Ferguson's men had their place in the Cup Final, to be played a week after the last game of the league, by beating Sheffield United, Wrexham, Leeds United and QPR, and Crystal Palace after a replay. The victory over Palace was overshadowed by the death of a Palace fan, killed in a fight between rival supporters outside a pub before the first match. In the replay, the players were warned to behave well in his memory and not to incite the crowd, but Roy Keane was sent off for violent conduct. "Once again United are in the dock," remembers Ferguson. "We got through the rest of the game and went back to the deadest dressing room I can remember. We were in the Final of the FA Cup for the second successive year and no one was celebrating. It was a nightmare come true."

So the last week of the season was set up for the double double. Unfortunately there were plenty more nightmares and precious little celebration at Old Trafford. Blackburn lost at Liverpool, but United could only draw 1-1 with West Ham. "We were battering them," complains Ferguson, "but it just wouldn't go in for the winning goal. I just don't know how we didn't get the ball into the net." A week later Everton beat United 1-0 in the Cup Final, thanks to some inspired goalkeeping by Southall and a goal by Rideout. "It was a disappointing day," says Ferguson. "I didn't think we deserved to lose. It's five years since we've won nothing. Sometimes our players forget what defeat is like. They know now. But we have played football, always entertained, we never shut up shop or wasted time. Anyone who has watched us this season has had their money's worth, and I'm proud to say that."

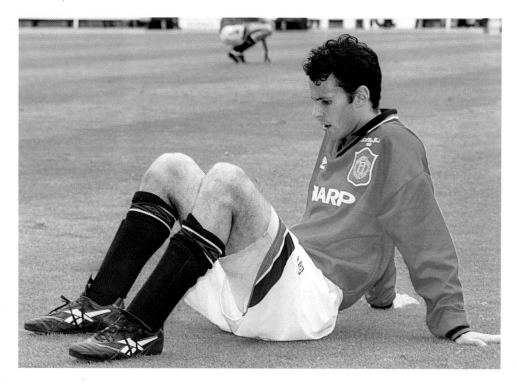

**Wembley:
the result sinks in.**

1994/95

Back row: Mark Hughes, Dion Dublin, Lee Sharpe, Eric Cantona, Keith Gillespie, Gary Pallister, Nicky Butt, Brian McClair, Chris Casper.
Front row: Andrei Kanchelskis, Peter Schmeichel, David May, Steve Bruce, Brian Kidd, Paul Ince, Ryan Giggs.

Premiership

Date		Opponent		Score	Scorers
Aug 20	(h)	QPR	W	2-0	Hughes, McClair
Aug 22	(a)	Notts Forest	D	1-1	Kanchelskis
Aug 27	(a)	Tottenham	W	1-0	Bruce
Aug 31	(h)	Wimbledon	W	3-0	Cantona, McClair, Giggs
Sep 11	(a)	Leeds U	L	1-2	Cantona
Sep 17	(h)	Liverpool	W	2-0	Kanchelskis, McClair
Sep 24	(a)	Ipswich T	L	2-3	Cantona, Scholes
Oct 1	(h)	Everton	W	2-0	Kanchelskis, Sharpe
Oct 8	(a)	Sheff Wed	L	0-1	
Oct 15	(h)	West Ham	W	1-0	Cantona
Oct 23	(a)	Blackburn	W	4-2	Cantona, Kanchelskis 2, Hughes
Oct 29	(h)	Newcastle U	W	2-0	Pallister, Gillespie
Nov 6	(a)	Aston Villa	W	2-1	Ince, Kanchelskis
Nov 10	(h)	Man City	W	5-0	Cantona, Kanchelskis 3, Hughes
Nov 19	(h)	Crystal P	W	3-0	Irwin, Cantona, Kanchelskis
Nov 26	(a)	Arsenal	D	0-0	
Dec 3	(h)	Norwich C	W	1-0	Cantona
Dec 10	(a)	QPR	W	3-2	Scholes 2, Keane
Dec 17	(h)	Notts Forest	L	1-2	Cantona
Dec 26	(a)	Chelsea	W	3-2	Hughes, McClair Cantona,
Dec 28	(h)	Leicester C	D	1-1	Kanchelskis
Dec 31	(a)	South'ton	D	2-2	Butt, Pallister
Jan 3	(h)	Coventry C	W	2-0	Scholes, Cantona
Jan 15	(a)	Newcastle U	D	1-1	Hughes
Jan 22	(h)	Blackburn	W	1-0	Cantona
Jan 25	(a)	Crystal P	D	1-1	May
Feb 4	(h)	Aston Villa	W	1-0	Cole
Feb 11	(a)	Man City	W	3-0	Ince, Cole Kanchelskis
Feb 22	(a)	Norwich C	W	2-0	Ince, Kanchelskis
Feb 25	(a)	Everton	L	0-1	
Mar 4	(h)	Ipswich T	W	9-0	Keane, Cole 5, Hughes 2, Ince
Mar 7	(a)	Wimbledon	W	1-0	Bruce
Mar 15	(h)	Tottenham	D	0-0	
Mar 19	(a)	Liverpool	L	0-2	
Mar 22	(h)	Arsenal	W	3-0	Hughes, Sharpe, Kanchelskis
Apr 2	(h)	Leeds U	D	0-0	
Apr 15	(a)	Leicester C	W	4-0	Sharpe, Cole 2, Ince
Apr 17	(h)	Chelsea	D	0-0	
May 1	(a)	Coventry C	W	3-2	Scholes, Cole 2
May 7	(h)	Sheff Wed	W	1-0	May
May 10	(h)	South'ton	W	2-1	Cole, Irwin
May 14	(a)	West Ham	D	1-1	McClair

Final League position: second in FA Carling Premiership

FA Cup

Round	Date		Opponent		Score	Scorers
3rd Round	Jan 9	(a)	Sheffield U	W	2-0	Hughes, Cantona
4th Round	Jan 28	(h)	Wrexham	W	5-2	Irwin 2, Giggs, McClair, Hughes
5th Round	Feb 19	(h)	Leeds U	W	3-1	Bruce, McClair, Hughes
6th Round	Mar 12	(h)	QPR	W	2-0	Irwin, Sharpe
Semi-Final	Apr 9		Crystal P	D	2-2	Irwin, Pallister
Replay	Apr 12		Crystal P	W	2-0	Bruce, Pallister
Final	May 20		Everton	L	0-1	

European Champions' Cup

	Date		Opponent		Score	Scorers
Group A, Game One	Sep 14	(h)	Goth'burg	W	4-2	Giggs 2, Sharpe Kanchelskis
Game Two	Sep 28	(a)	Galatasaray	D	0-0	
Game Three	Oct 19	(h)	Barcelona	D	2-2	Hughes, Sharpe
Game Four	Nov 2	(a)	Barcelona	L	0-4	
Game Five	Nov 23	(a)	Goth'burg	L	1-3	Hughes
Game Six	Dec 7	(h)	Galatasaray	W	4-0	Davies, Keane Beckham, Bulent

Taking

1995/96

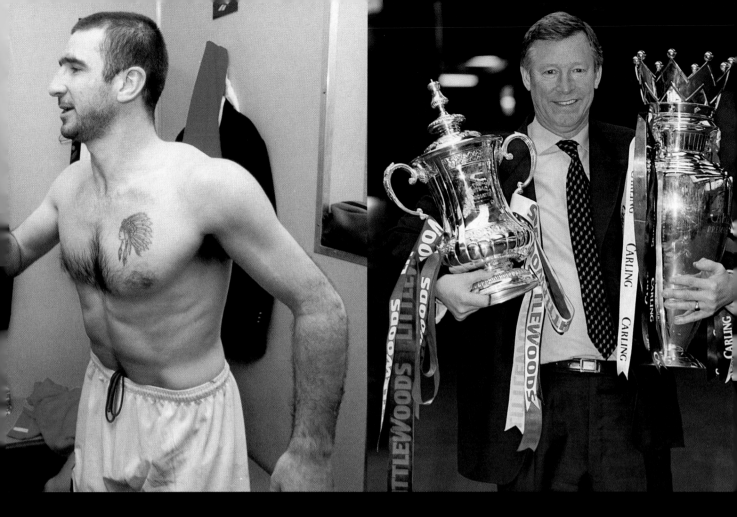

the crown

United fans were dismayed that in the summer of 1995, after the frustration of the previous season, Ferguson weakened his squad rather than strengthened it. He sold Andrei Kanchelskis, Paul Ince and Mark Hughes – Old Trafford heroes to a man – and didn't bring anyone in to replace them.

Ferguson says he had very little choice in the matter. "Mark Hughes was a legend, but his transfer was out of my hands really because he didn't sign his contract. Paul, I think, was hankering to go to Italy and he had it written in his contract that if an Italian club came in for him, he'd have the chance to go. So I think that all the hullabaloo, with Paul telling the fans that they're trying to sell me, doesn't wash too well now. I think people know the facts.

"More than a year before Kanchelskis left there were faxes going around saying he was available, and I find that amazing. I think he let the club down. During the conflict with Everton and ourselves he said: 'I've signed a five-year contract with Everton and that's binding.' So I told him 'Yes, and last year you signed a five-year contract with us and that's binding too.' But in the end that one was also out of my hands."

What the whole thing boiled down to was that United would have to rely, in some part, on the new batch of young players that were coming through the youth system. Indeed, Butt, Scholes and the Neville brothers were in the starting line-up for the first match against Aston Villa, with Beckham and O'Kane coming on as substitutes. The season could have started worse, but not much worse. Within 37 minutes Aston Villa were 3-0 up against an experimental five-man defence. United rallied in the second half to pull back to 3-1 with an 84th-minute goal by Beckham, but it was too little, too late. "You can't win anything with kids," said Alan Hansen on *Match of the Day* after the game. "I don't blame the young players. They were no more at fault than some of the older ones," said Ferguson at the time. "Alan Hansen's a pundit," he added later. "OK, he played football but I don't think he has the qualities to manage a football team and I think he knows he hasn't got them. He was a terrific player but he's not deep in his knowledge of the game. He gets a bit excited about Manchester United, maybe because of the old Liverpool thing. It affects him a wee bit."

Meanwhile the kids starting doing Ferguson proud. Paul Scholes was particularly effective: at one point in the autumn, he had scored eight goals in seven matches. United didn't look world beaters – but they were keeping in touch with leaders Newcastle.

The cup competitions were a different matter. One of the most humiliating days in United's history arrived when they were beaten 3-0 by York City at Old Trafford in the Coca-Cola Cup, and could only win 3-1 in the return, to go out of the competition. More painful for Ferguson was United's swift UEFA Cup exit, to Russian team Rotor Volgograd. United did the hard part well by getting a 0-0 draw in Russia – then blew it at Old Trafford. Peter Schmeichel's amazing last-minute header was enough to salvage some pride, and United's 39-year unbeaten record at home in Europe, but not the match which Volgograd won on away goals.

Again, United realised quite early in the season that they had to concentrate on winning the double. And this time they had Eric Cantona back in their side. Cantona returned to the fold on 1 October for the home match against Liverpool. What's more, he had the balls to take a second-half penalty, with United trailing. He scored, of course, to force a 2-2 draw.

The league campaign quickly became a two-horse race between Newcastle and United (with Liverpool coming up on the outside) and, for most of it, Newcastle was quite a few lengths clear. But some crucial results kept United within sight - not least their home and away victories against Keegan's men. Ferguson especially enjoyed the atmosphere in the match at St James' Park. "The Newcastle fans are tremendous. They concentrate on their own thing, they don't go on about Manchester United or the Munich air disaster. They sing their own songs. They wave their arms up and down. Newcastle fans are only interested in Newcastle United. We got a brilliant reception when we went up there, the support was fantastic towards us. They recognised we'd won an important game and we'd done well to win it."

The FA Cup wasn't going too badly, either, although United had to ride their luck a bit. In the first round they disposed of Sunderland at Roker Park, after having the worst of a draw at Old Trafford. An easy win at Reading was followed by a close shave against Manchester City. United equalised an early Rosler goal thanks to the dodgiest of penalties, before Sharpe volleyed them into the quarter finals. Southampton frightened United at Old Trafford, where they had a good-looking goal disallowed before Cantona and Sharpe scored in the second half. And United went a goal down to Gullit-inspired Chelsea in the semi finals, before rallying with two second-half goals in five minutes. Wembley beckoned… and the double looked a possibility, as long as United could win their race with Newcastle.

Most people reckon Newcastle threw away the League Championship in the last half of the season in 1995/96, but that doesn't take account of United's superb late-season form. From February onwards they won all but two matches. They failed to win at QPR, where they came away with a draw, and at Southampton where they played for half a game in their infamous grey kit. "When you defend as badly as we did, you are going to lose games," said Ferguson after the set-to at The Dell. "There is no doubt about that."

The "Leeds are cheating" fracas proved that Ferguson was coping with the pressure better than Keegan, and it rubbed off on his team. They cruised to a third League Championship in four years with a 3-0 victory over Bryan Robson's Middlesbrough.

"I think Newcastle did great," said Ferguson, after the season had finished. "They had a marvellous season. Fortunately for us, we got on a run at the right time, just as they were starting to lose a few games. I think it was that combination that did it: our run and the fact that they began to drop points. They had to have a blip, and when they did, we capitalised."

Ferguson thinks that it is no accident that United had the bottle at the end of the season which Newcastle seemed to lack. "In the end," beams Ferguson, "experience proved to be a telling factor. Having gone through the major disappointments of 1992 and 1995, we knew what to expect from the final nail-biting weeks of the season. Most of our players knew only too well the feelings they were hoping to avoid."

The FA Cup Final followed on 11 May and again United triumphed, throttling Liverpool's resolve before finishing them off with a Cantona coup de grace. "To be honest," says Ferguson "I thought it was an extra-time job. The funny thing is that coming so late, the goal killed Liverpool completely." Ferguson was criticised afterwards for closing down the game, but he was quick to defend himself. "It was unbelievable!" he raved. "One journalist I read – it was a terrible, disgraceful article for the *Guardian* – said he blamed me for a poor Final! Our attitude is always to win, and always to entertain, and it always has been. The point is, with Liverpool's system, it's hard to get the ball off them, and when we did get the ball it was very difficult for us to get it forward to Cantona."

Ferguson admits that winning the double double is his greatest achievement at Manchester United so far ("I still have to pinch myself"). He knows he couldn't have done it without that first Championship win in 1993. "I've got to recognise that winning the title the first time was one hell of an achievement. To get that albatross off your back opens the door to many things. It gives you control, gives you confidence, it forces belief and it develops ambitions that things can be done. Last season was the culmination of a lot of hard work: especially the development of the youth policy which began when I first came. The real achievement was how well and how long the young players lasted. That was an amazing thing."

1995/96

Back Row: Andy Cole, Brian McClair, Roy Keane, Gary Neville, David Beckham, Gary Pallister, Nicky Butt, Ryan Giggs, Eric Cantona, Brian Kidd.
Front Row: Phil Neville, Denis Irwin, Peter Schmeichel, Steve Bruce, David May, Paul Scholes.

Premiership

Aug 19	(a)	Aston Villa	L	1-3	Beckham
Aug 23	(h)	West Ham	W	2-1	Scholes, Keane
Aug 26	(h)	Wimbledon	W	3-1	Keane 2, Cole
Aug 28	(a)	Blackburn	W	2-1	Sharpe, Beckham
Sept 9	(a)	Everton	W	3-2	Sharpe 2, Giggs
Sept 16	(h)	Bolton W	W	3-0	Scholes 2, Giggs
Sept 23	(a)	Sheff Wed	D	0-0	
Oct 1	(h)	Liverpool	D	2-2	Butt, Cantona
Oct 14	(h)	Man City	W	1-0	Scholes
Oct 21	(a)	Chelsea	W	4-1	Scholes 2, Giggs, McClair
Oct 28	(h)	Middlesbro	W	2-0	Pallister, Cole
Nov 4	(a)	Arsenal	L	0-1	
Nov 18	(h)	South'ton	W	4-1	Giggs 2, Scholes, Cole
Nov 22	(a)	Coventry C	W	4-0	Irwin, McClair 2, Beckham
Nov 27	(a)	Notts Forest	D	1-1	Cantona
Dec 2	(h)	Chelsea	D	1-1	Beckham
Dec 9	(h)	Sheff Wed	D	2-2	Cantona 2
Dec 17	(a)	Liverpool	L	0-2	
Dec 24	(a)	Leeds U	L	1-3	Cole
Dec 27	(h)	Newcastle U	W	2-0	Cole, Keane
Dec 30	(h)	QPR	W	2-1	Cole, Giggs
Jan 1	(a)	Tottenham	L	1-4	Cole
Jan 13	(h)	Aston Villa	D	0-0	
Jan 22	(a)	West Ham	W	1-0	Cantona
Feb 3	(a)	Wimbledon	W	4-2	Cole, Perry, Cantona 2
Feb 10	(h)	Blackburn	W	1-0	Sharpe
Feb 21	(h)	Everton	W	2-0	Keane, Giggs
Feb 25	(a)	Bolton W	W	6-0	Beckham, Bruce, Cole, Scholes 2, Butt
Mar 4	(a)	Newcastle U	W	1-0	Cantona
Mar 16	(a)	QPR	D	1-1	Cantona
Mar 20	(h)	Arsenal	W	1-0	Cantona
Mar 24	(h)	Tottenham	W	1-0	Cantona
Apr 6	(a)	Man City	W	3-2	Cantona, Cole, Giggs
Apr 8	(h)	Coventry C	W	1-0	Cantona
Apr 13	(a)	South'ton	L	1-3	Giggs
Apr 17	(h)	Leeds U	W	1-0	Keane
Apr 28	(h)	Notts Forest	W	5-0	Scholes, Beckham 2, Giggs, Cantona
May 5	(a)	Middlebro	W	3-0	May, Cole, Giggs

Final League position: first in FA Carling Premiership

FA Cup
3rd Round

Jan 6	(h)	Sunderland	D	2-2	Butt, Cantona

Replay

Jan 16	(a)	Sunderland	W	2-1	Scholes. Cole

4th Round

Jan 27	(a)	Reading	W	3-0	Giggs, Parker, Cantona

5th Round

Feb 18	(h)	Man City	W	2-1	Cantona, Sharpe

6th Round

Mar 11	(h)	South'ton	W	2-0	Cantona, Sharpe

Semi-Final

Mar 31		Chelsea	W	2-1	Cole, Beckham

Final

May 11		Liverpool	W	1-0	Cantona

UEFA Cup
1st Round (1st Leg)

Sep 12	(a)	Rotor V	D	0-0	

Replay

Sep 26	(h)	Rotor V	D	2-2	

Fergie

Above, left to right:
Ferguson stands firm as Hughes, Kanchelskis
and Ince leave United.

on Fergie

Alex Ferguson has made mistakes – he admits as much – but nothing prepared him for the astonishing press coverage that marked the start of the 1995/96 season. "Fergie must Go" screamed the back page of the *Daily Star*, in a story based on a *Manchester Evening News* poll that claimed 53 per cent of United fans wanted Ferguson to leave.

True, star players Hughes and Ince had left the club and Kanchelskis was on his way. If you'd believed the "United in Crisis" newspaper stories, however, the man who'd brought the glory days back to United suddenly wasn't fit to manage a burger stand at Old Trafford, let alone the biggest football club in Britain.

What angered Fergie more than anything was that the whole poll was based on a handful of anonymous phone calls that might even have been made by Manchester City fans. "I was livid. I was absolutely infuriated. It angered me even more because it was the *Manchester Evening News*, and for nine years we've had David Meek's involvement with the club. I compromised myself with the nationals by giving the *Evening News* first-hand knowledge of what was happening at this club. But there can never be the relationship again that I had with David Meek. They've lost that. They'll never get anything that the rest don't get, they won't get anything special. I've done nine years of compromises with that paper and then they stick the knife in you. And now they won't get any marking of their cards, they'll just get straightforward news as the rest do."

Ferguson refuses to gloat over landing the double, but denies the loss of the three star players was a mistake. Hughes was out of contract and wanted to leave ("I could do nothing about that"), Ince was looking for a move to Italy and Ferguson was happy to let him go ("for the good of the team"), and Kanchelskis, he insists, was motivated purely by money and there was nothing he could do to stop him moving to Everton. In his early days at the club, however, he concedes that he made errors.

"At first," he explains, "it wasn't easy to cope with the learning curve at a club where I had to absorb so many lessons as I went. I coped on instinct, really. I called the shots I believed to be right, but wrong decisions were inevitable, I suppose. Up to seven or eight moves I made in that period proved later to be ill-advised. Nothing major, of course, but if I were overlooking the management side in the future it would be far easier nudging the new man in the right direction."

He says now that he believes he stuck with some of the older players too long when he arrived at the club. "I wanted to be fair and give everyone a chance to show me what they were capable of," he explains. Ferguson cites the example of Frank Stapleton. "His reputation was as long as your arm, but he had lost his mobility and he just didn't look as if he would ever score a goal."

Ferguson looks back to when he did bring new players in at the start of the 1989/90 season (Webb, Wallace, Ince, Pallister and Phelan) and, on reflection, he is critical of the way he went about it. "The introduction of five new players at once was not ideal. Maybe I should have done it when I first arrived at the club, when people would have been more prepared to wait a while before judging. Bringing them in when I did meant that for a large part of the season they were living in hotels and not enjoying the benefits of a settled life, while at the same time trying to come to terms with what being a Manchester United player really means."

He refutes criticism of his choice of players in these early transfers, however, insisting: "I think I've played the transfer market very well the whole time. I think I've known what I wanted to get with the money available. But when I first came I didn't have a lot of money, to be honest."

If there is one real source of disappointment in Ferguson's United career so far, it has been the performances in the European Cup. The three foreigners rule had a crippling effect on Ferguson's team – although some of his resulting team selections in trying to overcome it have been the subject of fairly intense criticism. In 1993, he dropped Mark Hughes from the team to face Galatasaray away, so that he could play both Eric Cantona and Ryan Giggs. The match finished 0–0, and Fergie commented afterwards: "Tactically I felt it was the right thing to do, but perhaps they knew then that they'd got the advantage."

Ferguson's team selection was also slated in the media after United's November 1994 débâcle in Barcelona. He played Englishman Gary Walsh in place of Peter Schmeichel and the stand-in keeper found himself plucking the ball out of the Nou Camp net no less than four times. Ferguson is adamant, however, that this was not the reason for the defeat. "There was no way you could point a finger at Walsh," he says. "Schmeichel would definitely have been beaten by three of the goals, anyway. It was a humiliating experience. I couldn't wait to get them off at half time, but then we let in another before the break and there was no way

Right: Gary Walsh tries to hold the fort against Barcelona.
Below: missing the League in 1994/95.

Left: David May hoists the
1996 Premier League trophy.
Opposite page:
Paul Ince's scissor-kick livens
up the 1994 Charity Shield
against Blackburn.

back. I have no complaints; world-class players like those at Barcelona are absolutely fantastic."

In the next match, away at Gothenburg, he picked David May at right back. May had a nightmare game which the Swedes won 3-1. "I thought about Gary Neville after his outstanding display the previous Saturday against Crystal Palace, but experience was going to be vital. Also, if I didn't play David May, it was sort of saying to him: 'You've just never done it here'. I couldn't really desert him that way. I had to give him support.

"The European Champions' League that year was a major disappointment," admits Fergie. "We were very naïve. A more negative approach would have got us into the next phase, but is it a crime to be positive? I think we should be more careful defending away from home, but not negative."

Ferguson was also criticised for leaving out Mark Hughes and playing Andy Cole on his own up front in the final game of the 1994/95 season at West Ham. It was a game they drew 1-1, but it would have given them the Premiership title had they won. However, had Ludek Miklosko not been in sensational form that day, those same critics might have been hailing the decision a masterstroke.

And what of Andy Cole? At the start of the 1995/96 season, Ferguson was quoted as saying: "I can't wait for Andy and Eric to get together next year. Andy will definitely get us 30 goals next season." Ferguson will never openly criticise any of his players, but he must be concerned that one might turn out to be an expensive mistake.

If it does, then it will be one of very few. For, as the sports editor of the *Manchester Evening News* is no doubt all too aware, Alex Ferguson's career at United is rapidly taking on legendary proportions... and that fact has got very little to do with luck.

Postscript

Ten glorious years. It's a remarkable story. A story of one man's obsession, one man's single-mindedness, one man's determination to succeed... but it is not yet complete. There is still one chapter to be written.

"Winning the European Cup would give me enormous satisfaction and complete my task as a manager," admits Ferguson. "I will not rest until I've done it. I feel that then everything I've worked for since coming down to Manchester United would all be worthwhile.

"If I look at my career, I would have to say: 'What did I do in Europe?' I have to admit that I've had a disappointing record in the European Cup, both at Aberdeen and here. So I've got to stretch myself, the players and the club to the maximum by attacking the European Cup again.

"I can't look on it as the albatross around my neck. I've achieved so many things, I should be grateful. But I'm the type of person who needs the challenge and I'll give it my best shot. We need to improve in Europe. But I honestly believe that if we get the proper preparation and improve tactically – the younger players in particular – then we've got a good chance of doing better in the Champions' League. It's something we shouldn't be afraid of: sometimes it's the fear itself that stops you from progressing."

And if he lands that last, elusive trophy? If the final challenge is met and surpassed, then what? Retirement? "It depends when it is, of course," he says. "I may have to wait until I'm 70. But I hate that word retirement. I don't like it all. I couldn't live without football, it would be unbearable – the unthinkable option, in fact.

"I certainly would like to think I have a job for life if I wanted it at United. My greatest wish is to shape the whole future of the club beyond being just the manager. It would be very difficult to go anywhere else, wouldn't it? But you never know in football, you never know in life. I want to stay here the rest of my life. But they've only offered me a four-year contract so I have to assume I've got to work before I'll get offered anything else."

In truth, getting Alex Ferguson to budge from his desk at Old Trafford would be about as easy as moving the whole stadium up the road with a fork-lift. And if he did walk out tomorrow, there would be one hell of a gaping chasm to fill.

"The foundations are here for many years to come," Ferguson reflects. "I hope that my contribution to the structure of the club will be recognised in the future."

Red boss in Red Square.